Becoming a Police Officer

Becoming a Police Officer

✦

An Insider's Guide to a Career in Law Enforcement

Barry M. Baker

iUniverse, Inc.

New York Lincoln Shanghai

Becoming a Police Officer
An Insider's Guide to a Career in Law Enforcement

Copyright © 2006 by Barry M. Baker

iUniverse books may be ordered through booksellers or by contacting:

iUniverse
2021 Pine Lake Road, Suite 100
Lincoln, NE 68512
www.iuniverse.com
1-800-Authors (1-800-288-4677)

ISBN-13: 978-0-595-38078-7 (pbk)
ISBN-13: 978-0-595-82448-9 (ebk)
ISBN-10: 0-595-38078-6 (pbk)
ISBN-10: 0-595-82448-X (ebk)

Printed in the United States of America

Contents

Introduction

Perhaps it's true that nobody likes a cop, but what a wonderful adventure it is. In 1971, I embarked on that adventure in the City of Baltimore, Maryland. I began my career walking a foot post where murder, robbery, and every variation of violence was the order of the day. For twenty years thereafter, I remained where I began. Of course, I eventually got four wheels beneath me and a blue light above me. The mobility of the radio car only exposed me to more of *man's inhumanity to man*. Early in my career, I dated a young woman who insisted I should leave the police department and find a *real* job. Fortunately, I chose the police department, and ten years later, I found a *real* woman.

In 1991, I was promoted to sergeant where I supervised a squad of fourteen patrol officers. In 1994, I was promoted to lieutenant. As a lieutenant, I served as a patrol shift commander and later as a special operations commander. I ended my career in 2004 as a detective lieutenant where I supervised three detective sergeants and sixteen detectives.

While all of my supervisory positions were most fulfilling, I look back fondly on those twenty years as a patrol officer. While constant exposure to murder, rape, and mayhem can have negative effects on some people, my experiences from those years only fortified my beliefs in fate and one's destiny. When a man tries to stab you several times, and he misses each time, it makes you wonder. When a man tries to shoot you, but he fails, because his heavy gloves prevent him from getting his index finger inside the revolver's trigger guard, giving you time to grab the gun, you feel blessed. When a man points a sawed-off rifle at you and pulls the trigger, and the gun misfires, you know you're blessed.

When I sat down to write *An Insider's Guide to a Career in Law Enforcement*, I soon realized that I wanted to give young men and women the best possible advice to help them avoid the pitfalls they'll encounter as police officers. Police departments are younger than ever before, and experienced leadership is sorely lacking. *An Insider's Guide to a Career in Law Enforcement* is not a collection of war stories; it is a serious discussion of issues which will make or break a police officer's career.

While the *An Insider's Guide to a Career in Law Enforcement* is invaluable for those contemplating a career in police work, it's a most informative and entertaining read that will appeal to anyone who is simply interested in police work, and the perils faced by police officers.

1

Are You Ready for a Career as a Police Officer?

…the best education on Earth

There is no other profession, occupation, or endeavor you could undertake where you'll experience the realities of life at their best and worst. If you keep at it long enough, you'll interact with every level of society, and you'll learn there's not a lot of difference among people regardless of their educational or economic achievements. People sit in classrooms for years trying to learn why people do the things they do. In the end, their education is nearly all based on theory and hearsay. As a police officer, you'll be a participant in, and an eyewitness to, the realities most people only read about. It's the best education on Earth.

…compassion…adventure

You must possess the elements of compassion and adventure to be a police officer. The proportion of these elements relative to the other will change as your career progresses. Your compassion will be tempered by the unbelievable deceit you'll experience, and the adventure will be tempered by some really scary, life threatening situations.

…entrusted with enormous power

As a police officer, you'll be entrusted with enormous power. You will routinely, and lawfully, deprive your fellow citizens of their liberty. More importantly, you may find yourself in a situation where you could be forced to take a human life. This power separates you from the rest of society. No other government official possesses the breadth and depth of authority as does a police officer.

1

…higher level of scrutiny

The weight of authority brings one particular burden. There's really no way to assess this burden until you've completed your training and you're thrown into the fray. You'll have a head start if you realize from the outset that you'll be held to a higher level of scrutiny than any other government official. Unlike other government officials, your behavior off-duty will be expected to mirror your on-duty behavior. You must be prepared to conduct your personal life with the same degree of discretion as your professional life.

…the true test

There's no way to know if you're truly suited to be a police officer until you experience the true test. That test will probably come during the first year of your career. It will be totally unexpected. You'll probably be alone, and you'll be attacked by a person armed with a deadly weapon sufficient to take your life. You will react, and your reaction will provide you with the answers to the test. It will be a terrifying experience, but the terror will test your ability to act soundly and decisively. As long as you take the person alive and uninjured, you'll be the only person grading your test. Your mind will be able to view the incident like a slow motion video over and over, and you'll never forget a single detail of it for the rest of your life. There will be a short period afterward where you'll evaluate whether or not to continue your career, but once you determine that you acted free of panic, you'll probably continue your career and be better for the experience.

…literacy helps

Police work is not limited to chasing and capturing criminals. In fact, all the chasing and capturing doesn't amount to much unless the police officer has the ability to communicate events in writing so that criminals can be prosecuted, so literacy helps. Now, don't let this requirement for literacy scare you, because police officers are, in fact, some of the worst at communicating events in writing. With all the hype about police departments hiring college graduates, I doubt you'd find many with degrees in English.

…longevity it's not

The Internet is a great source to go to when choosing a police department. The first thing you should notice is that nearly every police department is hiring. Another thing you should realize is that attrition for police officers is very high.

Even with the attractive salary and benefit packages offered by nearly all departments, it's safe to say that fewer than half continue their careers to retirement, so longevity it's not. Many people join only for the attractive salary and benefits while ignoring the true demands of the career, so the high attrition rate should not be surprising. If you're considering a career as a police officer based solely on the salary and benefits, you'd be better off, for the long run, seeking another vocation.

…indispensable character trait

If you're a person who thrives on attention and recognition, you could run into problems. While you'll find some police officers who will do just about anything to grab the credit for just about everything, you'll soon recognize these people and tire of them even sooner. An individual who craves constant recognition usually exudes reckless self confidence in everything he or she does. As a police officer, particularly a brand new one, this exercise of self confidence can lead to disaster. Self confidence is an indispensable character trait for a police officer, but you must realize that your self confidence is only as good as the knowledge and experience upon which it is built. If you understand that you're entering a twenty to thirty year ongoing learning experience, you'll do just fine, and your self confidence will never fail you.

…self satisfaction

If you thrive on self satisfaction, this is the job for you. Among all the aggravations and pitfalls you'll encounter during your career, you'll experience countless opportunities to affect the lives of countless people in so many positive ways. If you decide to become a police officer now, that decision will actually save lives in the future. You'll know when you save a life by the overt action you take. You'll never know how many lives you've saved by just simply being there. Either way, how much more self satisfaction could anyone desire?

2

Choosing a Police Department

...ability to compare

Nearly every police department has a web site giving you the ability to compare a limited number of things. Even if you've decided on a particular department, it's still a good idea to do some research. You're choosing a career, and you want to choose a department which is best for your long term commitment. While you should not choose a career as a police officer based solely on salary and benefits, these items are extremely important, and they should be second only in importance to your desire to be a police officer.

...comparisons are limited

Beyond the salary and benefits listed, comparisons are limited. You've got to remember that a department's web site is promotional as well as informational. You've simply got to separate the hype from the factual information. The hype usually consists of opportunities for advancement and specialized assignments.

...some red flags

When you're browsing web sites, you want to look for some red flags. Some police departments are hiring people with criminal records. When you see a requirement that reads, "no felony conviction," the department is saying that a felony arrest, or a misdemeanor conviction, will not necessarily exclude a person from being hired as a police officer. Everyone deserves the benefit of doubt, but one would hope that a person arrested for a serious crime would be scrutinized beyond the absence of a conviction. To be on the safe side, you might want to put those departments at the bottom of your list. That "thin blue line" that everybody talks about is also a life line.

…not everyone gets them

Another thing you might see is merit raises included in the salary package. Most departments have a graduated increase over several years bringing you to a top officer's salary. Merit raises tell you one thing…not everyone gets them. You often hear politicians talk about merit raises. Does that tell you anything?

…educational background

While most departments require only a high school diploma, some departments may offer a modestly higher salary to people with a four year college degree. Some of the nation's wealthiest jurisdictions may require all new hires to have a bachelor's degree as a minimum educational background. Many departments will have some sort of college tuition assistance for officers who work toward a college degree.

…practical benefit

If you already have a bachelor's degree, don't expect the degree to aid you when it comes to promotions and transfers. While police departments like to brag about the educational level of their officers, rarely, if ever, does the practical benefit of a degree to the individual officer mirror the department's hype. The biggest benefit of a degree is the absence of an excuse for denying you something you weren't going to get anyway.

…large department versus a smaller one

There is no question that you'll gain more experience in a shorter time on a large department versus a smaller one. If you really want to get in on the action, it's not a hard thing to figure out. If you join a large department in a city with a high crime rate, you'll find it relatively easy to get assigned, as a patrol officer, to a high crime area. Remember, police officers face the same challenges whether they be in a large department or a small one. Your rate of exposure to crime and criminals in a large department is simply a matter of greater frequency and volume.

…bewildered and confused

You might think that talking with police officers would be a good way to evaluate a department you're thinking about joining. Obviously, you'd have to talk with more than just a few officers to get a variety of viewpoints. Unfortunately, this exercise will probably leave you bewildered and confused. Police officers are used to conversing with people who aren't the least bit interested in what they've got to say. When you come along seeking their wisdom and direction, some will bombard you with negative input while others will view your interest with suspicion and ignore you. When, or if, you encounter an officer who gives you thoughtful and balanced advice, you'll probably view him or her with suspicion.

…your own observations

There really is no way for anyone to properly evaluate a police department from the outside. If you've been a long time resident of the jurisdiction where you intend to join the police department, you'll be familiar with that department's reputation. You may know members of the department who you can trust to give you a fair assessment of the department. You'll also be familiar with positive, or negative, publicity generated by the department, and you'll be able to assess the validity of publicity from your own observations.

…a career decision

Whatever means you use to choose a department, keep in mind that you're making a career decision. As a police officer, you will not have the flexibility to move in and out of police departments without, in most cases, losing valuable time and benefits. As a young officer, you won't be able to appreciate the value of those first few years of your career, so you'll just have to take what I'm saying on faith. Only at, or near, the end of your career will the value of those first years become evident to you. While some departments will offer experienced officers the opportunity to buy into their retirement systems and transfer a certain number of years' service, most do not. If you change departments during your career, and you throw away years of service, you will regret it.

3

Recruit Training

...amount of time

Once you're accepted for employment as a police officer, you'll enter a period of training. The length of the training will depend upon the jurisdiction; however, six months is usually the amount of time required by most departments. In most cases, new recruits will commute daily to training while some departments may require residence in a barrack style environment. A large department will likely maintain its own training academy, and recruits from smaller departments in the area will train along with recruits from the larger department.

...the uniform

You'll be issued uniforms, and you'll be required to wear the uniform at all times during your training. The uniform will probably be similar to the uniform worn by fully vested members of your department; however, your uniform will have some type of alteration to identify you as a recruit in training. The point in your training when you're issued your firearm will be determined by your department's training policy.

...don't take it literally

When you begin your training, you'll probably be sworn as a probationary officer and vested with full authority under the law. If this is the case, don't take it literally. Your instructors should make it very clear to you, on your very first day, that you are not to exert any authority over anyone. The only real authority you have as a recruit is over your own ability to look, listen, and learn. While technically, and for employment purposes, you may be designated as a police officer, you should never take any unsupervised enforcement action during your recruit status. At some point during your training, you'll be placed under the supervision of an experienced officer in the field for the purpose of experiencing enforcement situations.

…24 hours a day

It's very important to avoid any type of unsupervised enforcement action during your recruit training. The obvious exception would be an imminent, or in progress, life threatening situation. If you should be so unfortunate as to find yourself in such a situation, you'll have only your good judgement on which to rely. Things are rarely as they first appear to be, and your first option should always be the notification of on-duty police officers. While police officers are, technically, police officers 24 hours a day, departments frown on their officers taking enforcement actions while off duty. If a department discourages off-duty police enforcement by experienced officers, can you imagine the dim view it might take toward a know nothing recruit?

…put your enthusiasm on hold

It's relatively easy to avoid involvement in off-duty escapades. First, wear civilian clothing while commuting to and from the academy. Second, don't brag too much about your new profession. You should be proud that you've made it into the police academy and just as proud to wear the uniform. However, you're going to be wearing the uniform for a long time, so try to put your enthusiasm on hold until you're fully trained.

…example

Let's look at a totally probable example. You're in your first week of training, and you're driving to the academy. You stop at a red light, and you notice a man and two women standing on the sidewalk. You notice them, because the man and one of the women are involved in a heated argument. The argument is loud enough to cause some pedestrians to stop and listen to the exchange of domestic verbal abuse. The man and woman are not exerting any physical violence, and no threats of violence are being exchanged. The second woman is not involved in the argument, but she's standing close to the first woman as she looks around in all directions.

As you wait for the light to change, you hear a woman's voice shouting, "Officer, officer!" That's right, the woman who was looking all around spotted that police patch on the shoulder of your brand new uniform shirt. She runs over to you, and she immediately demands that you arrest her [expletive deleted] brother-in-law. If you were on-duty, and, if you were somewhat experienced, you'd probably do the following: You'd notify your dispatcher of your location and the nature of the incident. You'd then approach the arguing couple and separate them. You'd ease the most dynamic of the two to the side, and you'd engage him or her with calm conversation. It's always difficult to handle a domestic situation by yourself, but you'd probably be able to diffuse this situation since the argument had not escalated to physical violence.

Back to reality. You're not on-duty, and you're not yet even somewhat experienced. Your proper response would be to call 911. Maybe you've got a cell phone which would make things a lot easier. If you don't have a cell phone, your only option is to drive to the nearest donut shop and find a pay phone. Of course, if you drive off, the woman will get your license number, and she'll file a complaint against you for neglect of duty. Since you're new, eager, and stupid, you'll probably get out of your car and approach the couple. If you're lucky, things won't get any worse. If you're not lucky, things could get ugly. On the ugly side, just use your imagination.

…captive listener

A large portion of your training is going to consist of classroom instruction. A fair amount of your time is going to be wasted listening to guest lecturers who obviously despise police. Some of these lecturers will encourage debate; in which case, you should do your best to remain silent. Being a captive listener to ignorant, or even outrageous, views can be a positive experience so early in your career. After you graduate, you're going to be listening to stupid people everyday. If you've already learned to keep your mouth shut, you're well on your way to staying out of trouble. Remember, once you're performing your duties as a police officer, you never *debate* with anyone.

…particular attention

When it comes to the important instruction, listen very closely. You'll receive instruction on state and local laws; constitutional law; crime classification; crime reporting procedures; probable cause for arrests; arrest warrants; search and seizure warrants; rules of evidence; patrol and investigative procedures; use of force; firearms training; departmental rules and regulations, and much more. While everything is going to be important, pay particular attention to rules governing your personal conduct; use of force; probable cause, and all types of reporting requirements. If you're going to get into serious trouble, one or more of these four items will be involved.

…plum assignment

In a perfect world, all of your instructors would be top notch. Recognizing the obvious, some of your instructors will be exceptional while others won't even come close to meeting that standard. In any police department, an assignment to its police academy is considered to be a plum assignment. Like any other desirable specialized assignment, a police academy will receive its share people who get there for reasons having nothing to do with merit. An exceptional academy commander will be able to limit the damage to your instruction by assigning unqualified instructors to the most mundane systems' oriented tasks as possible.

…depth of experience

You'll be able to easily identify the exceptional instructors. They'll have a thorough knowledge and command of their subject, and they'll be able to share that knowledge with you in a smooth and natural manner. These instructors will be able to field any questions from recruits, because their command of the subject is derived from a real depth of experience. The less competent instructors will spend a lot of time bragging about their limited experiences. When recruits ask these instructors difficult questions, outside their limited pool of experience, they'll turn to their creative side, and they'll make up a response that may, or may not, be correct.

…displeasure for our company

There will come a time during your training when you'll be assigned to the field under the supervision of an experienced officer. When I did my training thirty plus years ago, we began weekend field assignments in our seventh week of training. We were permanently issued our Smith and Wesson revolvers the same week, and the academy spread us among the districts every Friday and Saturday night for the remainder of our academy training. The district shift commanders would assign us to their sector sergeants who would then assign us to their favorite, or less than favorite, officers. Some of the officers saddled with the extra weight were gracious and helpful while others promptly expressed their displeasure for our company.

…assortment of personalities

To this day, I would prefer that recruits be randomly assigned as we were assigned. We had the benefit of field training during peak crime hours supervised by a vast and varied assortment of personalities. It's true that such random assignments precluded an efficient process for the academy to evaluate our performance in the field, but it did give us a quick look at the complexities of police work. The real value of the random assignments was in our observations of how different officers navigated those complexities.

…Field Training Officer

Fast forward thirty years to the present, and you'll find that most larger departments conduct recruit field training under the supervision of a Field Training Officer (FTO). Under this system, you'll be assigned to an FTO for extended periods of time during your training. You'll work varied hours and weekdays to experience a wide variety of police functions. The FTO will have undergone academy training specifically designed for him or her to supervise you and evaluate your performance. In other words, your FTO is simply another instructor teaching you in the field. You should never forget that your FTO's evaluation of your performance is a significant part of your training, and poor evaluations could end your career.

…mirror image of the officer

In theory, a Field Training Officer program is an excellent way to provide you with stable supervision and provide the academy with an accurate evaluation of your progress under boredom and crisis. Like any other good system, there are always people around who can screw up a good thing. I can attest to the effectiveness of the FTOs' influence over their proteges since nearly all recruits will emerge from their field training as mirror images of the officers who trained them. This emulation of the FTO can be a good thing, or it can obviously be a bad thing if the FTO transfers bad habits to his or her recruit.

…steal it from someone else

Every police officer has his or her favorite areas of police work, and they'll naturally enhance their expertise in those areas. An FTO should avoid focusing on his or her favorite activities to the exclusion of others; however, it's a difficult thing to do since teaching what one knows best is an easier task. For example, you could finish your training as a veritable expert in traffic enforcement and drunk driving arrests, but you won't have the slightest idea how to handle a complaint of child abuse. The good FTO will make certain you handle every type of call available to you. Example…another officer is dispatched to a call for child abuse. Your FTO asks for the call to be reassigned to him or her so that you'll experience the benefit of handling the call. And so it goes…if you don't receive the call for something that's new to you, steal it from someone else.

…don't let it go to your head

Congratulations! You've successfully completed your academy training. You had knowledgeable instructors who provided you with accurate and comprehensive information. You got even luckier, and you had an excellent Field Training Officer who did his or her very best to familiarize you with as many different situations as possible in the time allotted to them. You should be proud of yourself, but don't let it go to your head. Now that you're on your own, you're going to find out just how much you don't know.

4

Patrol...Your First Assignment

...the backbone

Patrol is the backbone of a police department. This is an often stated belief by nearly all top police officials; however, once you become a police officer, you may come to question the sincerity of their belief. If you join a police department where the number one priority is providing a strong, well staffed, and well equipped patrol force, you've made an excellent choice. If you find yourself in a department where patrol shifts are continually short staffed, materiel resources are hoarded, because they are continuously in short supply, you've made a poor choice.

...more ways than you can imagine

A police department is its patrol force. Patrol officers are the department's uniformed presence in the community. Patrol officers are the first responders to protect life and property. Patrol officers are available, 24 hours a day, 7 days a week, to assist their fellow citizens in more ways than you can imagine.

...sleeping or partying

It's hard to say what kind of work schedule you'll encounter since schedules vary among departments. Some departments may have permanent volunteer midnight shifts while others rotate everyone through the midnight shift. Some may have permanent days off while others have a rotating leave schedule to afford everyone an equal number of weekends off. No matter what your work schedule is, you'll be working when the *normal* people are either sleeping or partying.

…can't handle the demands

A fair number of police officers are not successful as patrol officers. You'll see many tire quickly of the work schedule and the work. Even though the training has prepared them for the duties of a patrol officer, many just can't handle the demands of patrol duty. Some will resign. Some will stay on and perform with mediocrity while others will do everything in their power to find any position outside patrol duty.

…you'll cherish the independence

The key to being a successful patrol officer is your realization that you can get used to anything. All you need to do is recognize, and appreciate, the good parts and deal with the less than good parts. There aren't too many jobs where you're so independent from day one. In the beginning, that independence will be a little scary, because it takes time to build your knowledge and self confidence. As you become more comfortable with your abilities to solve problems, and act effectively, you'll cherish the independence.

…stepping stone

Just like most people, you've been programed from a very early age through television and movies to view real police as hot shot detectives. It's not surprising that many young people enter a police department looking at uniformed patrol as a mere stepping stone to a detective's badge. You probably expect to spend a year, two at the most, in uniform, before you move on to investigating the important stuff. Police recruiters don't help much when it comes to this misconception. Technically, a department may have a one or two year patrol requirement, before you can move to a specialized assignment, but that doesn't mean it's automatic.

…most important function

You should resist the perception that patrol is somehow less important than other assignments within a department since the opposite is true. Patrol is the single most important function of any police department. Patrol can, if necessary, assume any function of a specialized unit within a department, the same is not true in reverse. This concept is most obvious in a small department where everyone performs patrol duties as well as any specialized duties. In a large department, people in specialized assignments quickly become removed from the patrol function.

...resent the interruption

Whenever circumstances occur in a large department to cause specialized officers to temporarily return to patrol duties, the move is never smooth nor efficient. Departments often resort to putting as many officers as possible back into uniform to combat spikes in street crimes or to prevent year end crime numbers from adversely affecting crime reduction statistics. This practice is never smooth, because officers from the specialized assignments resent the interruption to their routine. The practice is inefficient, because the routine is interrupted. The effect on crime is minimal at best since the additional manpower is not integrated into the patrol function, and the work load on the regular patrol force is not reduced.

...where everything is learned

When you complete your training and enter the patrol force, you should view patrol for exactly what it is. Aside from being the core function of any department, patrol is where everything is learned. Some departments will limit a patrol officer's involvement in some investigations beyond the preliminary investigation which is the responsibility of the patrol officer. However, the initial stage of any investigation is always critical to its successful conclusion. Too many officers define preliminary as being synonymous with doing as little as possible. If you subscribe to this lazy man's thinking, you'll be of minimal value, and you'll learn even less. If you realize the absolute importance of your preliminary investigations, and you conduct every investigation with that realization, you'll solve a lot of crimes and learn a lot in the process.

...an entirely different animal

In most occupations or professions, you'd begin your career with an organization in a relatively low level position where your performance, and decisions, would have little impact, positively or negatively, on the organization or other people. Police work is an entirely different animal. From the very first day of your field deployment, you'll be saddled with responsibilities too numerous to list. On your very first day, you could literally have to make a life or death decision. Your first months as a patrol officer will not be easy. No matter how much training you've received, it won't fully prepare you for the multitude of circumstances you might experience.

…frequently hostile

As a brand, spanking, new officer, the most important knowledge you can possess is the knowledge of your ignorance. While youth should be cherished, youth, and the inexperience that comes with it, will be your biggest enemies. When you put on that uniform, you'll be expected to possess a level of wisdom not even expected of judges. While judges can pass off anything for wisdom in the totally controlled environment of a court room, your environment will be totally unpredictable and frequently hostile.

…don't do it

In those first months, and beyond, a good axiom to follow is, "When in doubt, don't do it." In the beginning, you'll encounter situations where you know you have to arrest a person; even though, you might not be certain under what legal basis you'll be acting. Your common sense, combined with your training, will carry you through on the obvious situations. In the less than obvious situation, your decision to do nothing may be your most reasonable course of action. In other words, every enforcement action you take will have consequences. You want to be certain the consequences will land on the person you arrest and not on you.

…learning process

If you join a police department, because you really do want to be a police officer, it's going to be enormously difficult to restrain your enthusiasm. You're going to want to experience as much as you can as fast as you can. Right from the beginning, patrol puts you front and center in the action. In the beginning, you need to temper your enthusiasm with the knowledge that you are just at the entry stage of a very long learning process.

5

Specialized Assignments

...could mean anything

A specialized assignment in a police department could mean anything outside the normal duties of a patrol officer. Obviously, a large department will have more positions for specialization than a smaller one. I think most young people entering police work probably view detectives as the most prominent example of a specialized assignment; even though, your department may have numerous areas of specialization.

...if it has one

Part of a department's promotional hype may include your opportunity to become a detective. If you're really that interested in becoming a detective, you should check out the department's process for a detective assignment...if it has one. The trouble with being young will be your ignorance with the ways of the world. Just because you'd like to be a detective, or even if you're qualified to be a detective, doesn't mean you will be a detective.

...government is different

A common misconception you may have is the idea that an assignment to a specialized activity will come sooner than later if you work hard toward that goal. That may be true in private industry where competence and hard work is essential to the bottom line, but government is different. In a police department, it's who you know, and who knows you, that makes the difference. If you happen to be competent and hard working, that's just a plus for you and the specialized unit where you're assigned.

…chosen members

If you're a woman, or a member of a racial minority, you might think you'll stand a better chance for a specialized assignment. It's true that your department will be sensitive toward maintaining gender and racial balances within specialized units. Years ago, when there were few members of a department falling into either the former or latter group, your sex or ethnicity would have been a tremendous advantage for you. Today, however, the numbers of women and racial minorities are sufficient to erase that advantage. In other words, that "good ole' boy" system that everybody cries about has simply been expanded to include chosen members of both groups.

…farthest thing from your mind

The good news is that it will be the same wherever you go. Furthermore, when you join a police department, entering a specialized assignment should be the farthest thing from your mind. You'll hear officers, with all of two years' experience, complaining about how burned out they are, and it's time they should be assigned to some specialized unit. Put those officers on your don't get to know list. If they're burned out after only two years, they're just looking for a desk to use for a foot rest.

…important thing to remember

You'll start your career as a patrol officer, and you may even end your career as a patrol officer. If you spend twenty years or more in that radio car…congratulations, because there are not that many people tough enough to handle the day to day rigors of patrol for such an extended period of time. The important thing to remember is that the more time you spend as a patrol officer, the better prepared you'll be for any type of specialized assignment.

6

Promotions

...the best opportunity

Before you join any police department, you should make yourself familiar with the department's promotion process. If you end up making a career out of police work, you want to give yourself the best opportunity to advance in the ranks.

...the rank structure

Most departments use military rank designations: corporal; sergeant; lieutenant; captain; major; lieutenant colonel; colonel. The chief's rank may be designated by four stars, and his or her deputy may be three stars. Rank designations among departments vary. Some may have various sergeant ranks, and the chief may wear a colonel's insignia. However, the sergeant and lieutenant ranks are relatively universal in the rank structure. The sergeant is the first line of supervision, and the lieutenant is the first line of management.

...trash it

In your search for a department, you want to make certain you join a department that gives you a fair opportunity for promotion. At some point in every department's rank structure, promotion becomes a purely political process. You want a department with a civil service promotion process which gets you as far up the rank structure as possible. Most departments should include the rank of lieutenant under civil service. If the department you're looking at doesn't, trash it, and go on to the next one.

...process for promotions

While most departments list requirements for promotion, they probably won't describe the process for promotions. Before applying to a department, you should contact the civil service commission in that jurisdiction to learn the process for the department's promotional examinations. For example, a civil service examination should be required for promotion to sergeant and lieutenant before higher appointed positions are made by the police chief. Normally, the higher ranks of a police department are appointed positions drawn from the highest civil service rank, and those appointed serve at the pleasure of the police chief. Your main concern should be your ability to competitively aspire to the highest civil service rank.

...a chink in the civil service armor

There is sometimes a chink in the civil service armor. Civil service promotional examinations are pretty straight forward to a point. The examination usually consists of a written examination followed by an oral interview. You need to know the weight given to each portion of the examination. Obviously, 20% written and 80% oral should send up a red flag. Secondly, you need to know what, if any, restrictions apply to the Police Chief when selecting candidates from the final scored civil service list.

...two examples

Let's take two examples: The Police Chief has a list of 80 candidates eligible for promotion to sergeant. Candidates are listed 1 through 80 based on their combined written and oral scores. Sounds like an easy task for the Chief. Not so fast. This Chief has no restrictions, and the Mayor's driver is number 80. Do you think the Chief will promote the Mayor's driver over higher scoring candidates? You better believe it.

Second example: This Chief also has a list of 80 candidates, but this Chief is restricted on how he or she can choose promotions from the list. This Chief cannot skip more than four candidates in numerical order without going back to promote one he or she previously skipped. In other words, unless the Chief promotes at least 75 other people from the list, the Mayor's driver is out of luck this time around.

...it's just the way it is

It doesn't sound fair, does it? Well, it's just the way it is. Police Departments are government entities, and politics are politics. Any system that can be corrupted will be corrupted. Your task is to identify a department that has as many safeguards as possible in place. If you're a person who's already well connected in local politics, or, if you're an obsequious person who excels in the back stabbing art of politics, a fair civil service process could be a hindrance to you. However, if you're a competitive individual, with an arcane belief in merit, you want to choose a department that has a relatively fair process for advancement.

7

Never, Ever Lie

...the most important character trait

Truthfulness is the most important character trait affecting your career. As a police officer, your word is the most valuable thing you own. Even liars have a grudging respect for a police officer who doesn't lie.

...your word will be the only evidence

You obviously know you'll be dealing with some of the worst elements of society. One thing that all criminals have in common is lying. It's really quite understandable since telling the truth would certainly land them in jail. Your job will be to counter lies with truth and develop evidence to establish that truth. Many times your word will be the only evidence available.

...appreciative for good advice

From the outset, you'll be making decisions based on law, and you're going to make mistakes. You might not like to think you will, but you will. In most instances, you'll have the benefit of guidance from supervisors and fellow officers. Such guidance can, and will, be extremely helpful to you, and you should always be appreciative for good advice. Nobody likes a know-it-all. If you project a know-it-all attitude, you'll soon find the availability of helpful advice in short supply, and those mistakes I mentioned will only multiply.

...not all advice is good advice

On the other hand, not all advice is good advice. Even as a new officer, you should be a person with the ability to reason. Unless you're already a pathological liar, you'll instantly recognize advice, or direction, that is putting you in a position to be untruthful. Police officers become involved in some complicated situations, so advice can be given to you by another who misunderstands the details of the incident. Never be shy about pointing out misunderstandings.

Once you're sure the person understands the details, and that person still advises you to take an untruthful position, you should politely thank the person for the advice, and never seek advice, or guidance, from that person again.

…lies are lies

If you assume you need to maintain good working relationships with your fellow officers, you're absolutely correct in that assumption. However, maintaining good relationships does not mean you have to lie or have complicity in lies. Big or small, lies are lies. Your worst nightmare should be finding yourself in a position where you've lied, or condoned the lie of another, and the lie is exposed. At best you're simply branded as a liar. At worst, you'll go to jail as well as open yourself to civil liability.

…legal lying

Lies are all around us everyday and in everything we do. As a police officer, you'll become familiar with the word subterfuge. Subterfuge is lying to a person you're interrogating, or interviewing, for the purpose of revealing truth. This form of legal lying is only a ruse, and you should always document the details of any subterfuge you use during the course of an investigation. If you don't, you can be assured that a competent defense attorney will try to taint your integrity with any undocumented subterfuge. For that matter, the defense attorney will try to taint you with documented subterfuge; however, your up front truthfulness about the subterfuge should prevent any damage to your integrity.

…less than fair play

Subterfuge can be a double edged sword, and your documentation of subterfuge is all important to protecting your integrity and clearly separating fact from fiction in your investigation. Your use of subterfuge is not normally a big deal for a judge, but juries can be a different matter. Juries expect to hear lies attributed to defendants; however, when they hear lies attributed to police officers, even the harmless, and frequently necessary, lies associated with subterfuge can be problematic. Even when a jury fully understands the legality of the subterfuge, they often view it as synonymous with trickery and somewhat less than fair play.

…little loyalty to total truthfulness

Lying *to* a bad guy is totally opposite to lying *on* a bad guy; never the less, you'll find yourself working around some officers who believe that the ends always justify the means. You'll soon realize why some officers feel little loyalty to total truthfulness when you see so many criminals escape justice for any number of reasons. When some of those reasons can be nullified by a little lie here, or a little omission there, some officers will succumb to the temptation. Then, there are others, fewer thankfully, who are just pathological liars, and you won't be sure when they're telling the truth about anything.

…immune from corruption

From day one, your number one goal must be the preservation of your integrity. If you falter just one time, your integrity is lost. Never feel pressured to lie on anyone no matter how repugnant that person might be. While truth will not always achieve the proper ends, it is indestructible and immune from corruption.

8

The Police Report

...foundation for a police department

If cement is the foundation for a skyscraper, the police report is the foundation for a police department. A police department without a sound and efficient reporting system will translate into a corrupt and inefficient organization. Hopefully, the department you choose will have the leadership that recognizes this fact. Unfortunately, you will not be able to gauge your department's reporting standards; until, you become intimately involved with the reporting system.

...one criteria you can use

There is one criteria you can use to rate departments prior to employment. Violent crime is the mainstay of every department, or I should say the *reduction* of violent crime. If a department reports a yearly violent crime reduction in high single digit percentages, you should be suspicious. If a department reports the reductions in double digit percentages, you can safely consider such reporting as fiction.

...rolls down hill

Crime reduction is the most important measure of a police department's success. Politicians and police executives are constantly under enormous public pressure to reduce all crime and violent crime in particular. This pressure is one of those things that rolls down hill. As a police officer, it all starts with you. When a crime is reported to you, the police report you prepare is the official record of that crime.

…the "Bull Shit Theory"

We've got to get this one out of the way really quickly, because if you fall into this line of categorizing crime, you're going to do victims and yourself injustice. I call this the "Bull Shit Theory," and you're going to hear it time and again from new and experienced officers alike. If you're not careful, you're going to start thinking that a crime victim should fall into one of two categories…the deserving and the undeserving.

An undeserving victim could be an attractive female college student robbed at gunpoint while a deserving victim could be a female street prostitute who is brutally beaten and raped at gunpoint. While both crimes are Part 1 violent crimes under the FBI's Uniform Crime Reporting system, you'll soon learn that many officers will quickly dismiss the latter crime as, "that's bull shit."

Understand this. Most violent crime is committed against persons that many officers consider to be deserving victims. The reason is very simple. Most violent crime victims live in neighborhoods with high rates of violent crimes. Many victims are, themselves, involved in some sort of criminal activity. Just as simple is your job to accurately report crime no matter the social status of your victim.

…one of three ways

You're going to come into contact with a report of crime one of three ways. You'll be sent to a location by your dispatcher for a report of a crime; you'll be stopped on the street by a crime victim, or you'll ride up on a crime in progress. Crimes you observe in progress will, or should, get the attention they deserve; however, the reports could be a different matter.

…just doesn't sound right

You will, on occasion, have a crime reported to you that just doesn't sound right. It's your job to ask questions. Every police officer is an investigator. If something doesn't sound right, ask the question to clear up the issue. You'd be surprised how many officers fail to ask pertinent questions. As a new officer, your failure to ask the right questions can be excused to your inexperience. An experienced officer's failure to conduct a thorough interview of a crime victim is just plain laziness, incompetence, or both. Even as a new officer, you'll soon be able to recognize a senior officer who conducts a thorough and competent interview.

…the lies will become evident

When you encounter a victim whose account doesn't sound believable, press the victim for details. Do not immediately state your disbelief of the victim's account. The victim could be just excited and confused, and a calm and detailed interview could clear up any inconsistencies. During your interview, ask the same question more than once. If a victim is lying about all, or any part of the alleged crime, the lies will become evident.

…real interest in accurate crime reporting

If you're working in a department with lax reporting standards, you're going to see many, many, many reported crimes classified as *Unfounded*. In departments that have a real interest in accurate crime reporting, you'll be required to justify unfounded findings in writing. If the department reports its crime to the FBI, you'll be required to adhere to the UCR reporting criteria for an unfounded crime. The unfounded criteria is clear. You must prove the crime reported never occurred. The easiest way to prove that a crime is unfounded is for the victim to admit that he or she fabricated the offense.

…"that's the man who raped me"

During your career, you'll be approached by a person who will point to another person. Your person will say, "that's the man who robbed me at gunpoint," or, "that's the man who raped me." Both crimes are serious felonies, and both identified suspects would be subject to immediate arrest. Further, as eyewitness identifications go, they don't get any better. Once you have the suspect safely in custody, you're going to get further details from the victim. In most instances the victim is going to tell you that the crime in question was previously reported to the police. At this point you're going to feel pretty good about everything.

…you find an *Unfounded* report

With your suspect in custody, you're going to pull the original offense report and continue the investigation. Just one problem. You find no report at all, or you find an *Unfounded* report. If there's an unfounded report, it probably won't get any better. The unfounded report could be a one liner stating, "Unable to locate a victim/complainant." In all probability, the report will be false. Since the original officer couldn't prove the crime was unfounded, the officer took the easy way out by just saying no victim could be located.

...a couple of problems

You'll soon learn that you'd never want to be a victim and have to report a crime to some of the officers who work around you. That said, now you have a couple of problems. First, you have to reinvestigate the entire incident for which you've deprived a person of his freedom. It would simplify everything if the report did turn out to be unfounded, but that won't be likely. Second, you should contact the author of the unfounded report. You'll probably get the, "Ah, that was bull shit" response. Even if you're a new officer, don't be shy about expressing your displeasure to any practitioner of the "Bull Shit Theory."

...it's not your problem

Once you've established that your victim is credible, your report should be written under the original case number as the unfounded report. No matter what the unfounded report contains, you don't want to give the appearance of covering up anything. If a false police report does exist, it's not your problem beyond the fact that it could damage the case against your suspect. Your reporting should clearly, and accurately, explain the chronology of events. You don't have to go into details of the original officer's incompetence; that incompetence will be evident enough.

...failure to document

It's absolutely impossible to prepare you for all the weird circumstances you're going to encounter as a police officer. Your entire career is going to consist of trial and error. If you learn from your errors, you'll see the errors decrease dramatically over time. One of the most repeated errors officers make is their failure to document...document...document. Some officers spend more time avoiding writing a report than the time it would take to write one.

...lame and lazy excuse

One of the most often used excuses for not writing a report is, "the victim didn't want to make a report." Think about this for a moment. The victim called the police. The victim described the crime committed. The victim's description contained all the elements of the crime. Dah...the crime has already been reported. It is now your responsibility to *document* the occurrence of that crime. Sadly, experienced officers use this excuse often, and you must never adopt this lame and lazy excuse.

…write something

If you get into the habit of writing more than less, you'll experience far fewer problems during your career. Many of the situations you handle will not require writing a report, but there will be those times when you hear a little voice telling you to write something.

…example

Let's look at this example: You're dispatched to investigate a suspicious vehicle parked in front of a particular residence. There is no description of the vehicle. You arrive and find no vehicle parked in front of the home. You ask your dispatcher to identify the caller, and you learn that the call was made, anonymously, from a pay phone in the next block. You knock on the door of the residence, and a woman answers. She did not call police, and she knows nothing about a vehicle that may have been parked in front of her home. When you ask the woman if she's had any problems with anyone recently, she responds that she was an eyewitness to a murder some months earlier, and she's due to testify in the trial which has not yet been scheduled. You ask if she's received any threats, and she tells you she's received no threats of any kind.

At this point, most officers would simply clear the call and go back into service. You, however, go to the pay phone where you observe two young men sitting on a bench near the phone. They tell you they know nothing about anyone making a call at the pay phone. The men appear uncomfortable as you question them, but they comply when you request identification.

It's reasonable to say that you did everything you could with the information you had. You started with very little, and you ended up with very little. Your department will provide a report format for miscellaneous incidents, so why not write a report? In this instance, most officers would say to you, "It's a waste of time…there's nothing to it…it's bull shit."

You write the report, and you describe exactly what you did, and you identify everyone you interviewed. When your sergeant reviews your report, the sergeant might even ask, "Why did you write a report on this? You didn't have to write a report." The rest of your shift is uneventful, and you go home looking forward to two days off.

The next evening you sit down to watch the eleven o'clock news. The top news story is a home invasion where four people were murdered. One of the victims is the woman you'd interviewed the previous evening. In this example, you've probably already realized the significance of the woman being a state's witness to a murder. While murder is a big deal, the murder of a state's witness is a very big deal. In this example, your decision to write a report was made when you learned the woman was a state's witness.

When investigators uncover your response to the woman's home, some top brass will be disappointed when they're shown your report while others will see the positive aspect to your reporting. Police are just as skeptical toward other police as they are toward criminals. With the information available for this example, most police officers wouldn't have even knocked on the woman's door. Had your efforts in this instance not been documented prior to the murders, you'd be in for a grilling.

…off the hook

Whenever something really bad happens, and prior police response is revealed, command officers and supervisors will *always* initially assume that the responding officer(s) failed to take appropriate action. It's just how police think. If you're the officer involved, and there exists a written report confirming you did take appropriate action under the prevailing circumstances, you'll be off the hook. Your verbal confirmation of your appropriate action after the fact will carry little weight.

…omitting an established element

As I mentioned earlier, the reduction of Part 1 crimes is the top goal of any police department. Undoubtedly, at some point, a supervisor will tell you to reinvestigate a crime you've properly classified as a Part 1 crime. The supervisor may, or may not, enunciate the "Bull Shit Theory," but he or she will make it clear that the crime should be downgraded to a lesser offense. The only way the downgrading can be accomplished is by omitting an established element(s) of the crime already contained in your reporting. A good supervisor will never give you such direction, so you shouldn't feel badly when you refuse to lie by omission.

…wonder what hit you

Aside from the obvious physical dangers you'll encounter as a police officer, countless other dangers threaten you from within the very system you serve. You could find yourself in the wrong place at the wrong time, and you'll wonder what hit you. The police report is your best insurance against becoming a sacrificial lamb. Remember, you write complete and accurate reports for *everything* that requires reporting, and you let the little voice in your head guide you the rest of the way.

9

The Traffic Accident Report

...relatively simple to relatively complicated

Most police officers are not fond of filling out traffic accident reports. A department's accident report can range from being relatively simple to relatively complicated. Some reports are standardized statewide to facilitate the collection of statistical information. Whether the report is simple or complicated, police officers, in general, don't see the need for preparing a report for an accident that does not result in *obvious* serious injury or death. There is one exception to this view even for officers most adverse to writing accident reports. When the individual officer is involved in a traffic accident with his or her personal vehicle, no matter how minor, he or she will always base the validity of that view depending upon who is at fault.

...working for insurance companies

Investigating an accident and preparing a report can be time consuming, and officers have always complained that their time would be better spent combating crime instead of working for insurance companies. It took years, but police leadership finally listened, and many departments no longer require an accident report under certain circumstances. When you tell a police officer he or she doesn't have to write a report under certain circumstances, one can be assured those circumstances will be expanded way beyond those originally intended.

...report was critical

Imagine yourself driving down a two lane, one way street. You're traveling in the left lane as a car traveling in the same direction comes parallel with you in the right lane. As you cross an intersection, the car to your right inexplicably turns into you. The collision sends your car heading straight for a building at the corner of the intersection. As your front wheels strike the curb, you prepare yourself

31

for your head on collision with the building. Luckily, the impact with the curb changes the direction of your car, and you grab your steering wheel as you find yourself careening down the sidewalk. When you come to a stop, you pause for a moment to reflect on what force spared you from crashing into the front of that building.

Both cars are disabled, and the woman who crashed into you is complaining of serious injury to her back. Police and paramedics arrive. The paramedics promptly carry the woman off to the hospital, and you wait for the police officer to conduct his investigation. Two officers approach you as you stand ready with your driver's license and registration in hand. However, instead of asking you for the documents, one of the officers begins to explain the police department's policy on accident reports. As the first officer explains why no report will be written, the second officer is staring at you intently.

Since you're a member of the same police department, you're familiar with your department's written directive on accident reports. The officer concludes his totally bogus explanation, and you're about to educate him on the correct policy when the second officer waves his finger toward you and asks, "You're a police in the Eastern District, aren't you?" As you nod, the second officer quickly responds, "We'll write a report."

As you might expect, I wasn't overwhelmed with confidence in these officers to conduct a thorough investigation. To my surprise, the report was well done, and, most importantly, it contained complete identification and contact information for the witnesses to the accident. The report was critical since that poor woman who hurt her back obviously suffered a brain injury as well. Her fairy tale description of the accident to her insurance company, in the absence of facts contained in the report, would have made the whole incident more inconvenient than it already was.

…discretion will be abused

Think about how many times, during your travels, you happen upon the scene of a homicide, a bank robbery, or some other *real police* activity. Compare the number of those observations to the number of times you pass the scene of a traffic accident. Police departments are always looking for ways to improve their relations with the community. For a lot of people, the only time they'll need your assistance, and expertise, is when they're involved in traffic accidents. Why would a department create a policy giving discretion to officers when the leadership of the department must realize the discretion will be abused? The answer isn't that difficult. Police leadership will never personally be victimized by the misuse of that discretion.

…done an injustice

There will be times when you respond to a call for a traffic accident only to determine that no accident occurred. In order to have a traffic accident, there must be a motor vehicle involved, personal injury or a claim of personal injury, property damage, or both. A common example of this could occur when a vehicle simply bumps the bumper of another vehicle. Your investigation reveals no damage, and there is no claim of personal injury. Ergo, there is no traffic accident.

During my career as a patrol officer, I got into the habit of writing a miscellaneous incident report listing the incident as a 'Traffic Mishap" when my investigation revealed that no accident occurred. On one occasion, I received a civil court witness summons for a non-accident which occurred over a year earlier. While my recollection of the incident was vague, my report confirmed the absence of injury or property damage. At the conclusion of my testimony verifying the contents of my report, the Judge remarked that this was the first time he'd seen such a report. He went on to ask if the report was a standard policy within the police department? When I replied that it was not, the Judge remarked, "It should be."

Had I responded to that court appearance armed with only a poor recollection of the incident, everyone would have assumed that I had simply been negligent in my investigation of the alleged traffic accident. The plaintiff would have probably prevailed, and the defendant would have been done an injustice.

…save a lot of people a lot of aggravation

You'll find that traffic accidents produce liars on a nearly one to one ratio. When you respond to the scene of an accident, no matter how minor, just put yourself in the shoes of the unfortunate person whose only fault is being in the wrong place at the wrong time. The time you take to establish facts, and document those facts, will save a lot of people a lot of aggravation.

10

Police and Computers

...typing skills

If you're a young man or woman starting your police career, chances are you're familiar with computers. Most importantly, you're familiar with the keyboard. Hopefully, you use all your fingers when typing. If you're one of those two finger typists, take a typing course right now. Just knowing how to type will not make you a good police officer, but it will make your life much easier. Ten years ago, hand printing a report or other document was fine. Today, most departments are becoming more and more computerized, and your typing skills will be a significant key to your success.

...business goes on as usual

We live in a truly wonderful age of computer information technology. Since information is so important to police work, one would think this constantly improving technology would make police departments some of the most efficient organizations on earth. Well, not so fast. First, a police department is an entity of government, and government has never been known for its efficiency. When private profit making businesses purchase information technology, the technology works, or the businesses goes out of business. In government, if the technology doesn't work, business goes on as usual.

...only a fraction

Technology is not the problem. Sure, there are technical glitches that occur, and those are usually beyond most of us to understand, but the real problem lies with the people who are using the technology. Most of us comprehend only a fraction of the potential within modern computer software. This is reasonable since we're looking at a product created by genius. While the creators of software

are smart, the people who market the software are even smarter. When you match the marketers against politicians, and police executives, it's game over.

…paperless information system

No, the marketers are not the bad guys. With rare exception, when a police department purchases an information management system, it receives a system designed to deliver as promised. The big disconnect, between the marketer and the police, occurs with the day to day operation of the system. Police executives are fond of the phrase, "a paperless information system." Well, anyone who has progressed from the typewriter to word processing knows that just the opposite is true. Ten years ago, a published procedure for a particular activity might consist of two pages. Today, that same procedure might run to ten pages. That's why you'll see most of your department's procedures so lengthy and detailed. So much so, it will be impossible to follow all procedures consistently.

…the easy part

At this point, I'm only talking about word processing which is the easy part of any information system. It's so easy, in fact, that police executives abuse it with impunity. A police department is sensitive to the community; media, and politicians. When you do something that somebody in the community doesn't like, that person might contact the media. If the media finds it to be newsworthy, which doesn't necessarily mean it is, a story is created. If a politician is sensitive to anything, it's the media. The politician will waste no time getting on the phone to the police chief. Let's say that whatever you did was not wrong in any way. Without being able to punish you, the only alternative is to create a new written procedure.

…synonymous with lengthy

The task of producing a written procedure will fall to an administrative officer; sergeant, or lieutenant. The person who's assigned this task will want to exhibit his or her vast knowledge and ability to produce a comprehensive procedure. In this instance, comprehensive is synonymous with lengthy. No matter how mundane the procedure might be, the procedure's author will have you performing more steps than would be required for a far more serious activity. At some point, however, all your department's written procedures will be redone, or amended, to the point where you'll be physically unable to adhere to all the requirements all of the time.

…won't even know they exist

You, and everyone else, will take shortcuts out of necessity, because some written procedures will be just too much for the time involved. That said, you should always make every effort to follow every procedure in detail. Just because everyone condones the shortcuts will not help you if you find yourself under investigation for failing to follow a procedure to the letter. It gets even worse. Word processing has created so much paper, there will undoubtedly be directives and procedures in such volume that you, and most others, won't even know they exist.

…the good thing

Here's the good thing about word processing. It gives you the ability to document events in detail. Even good police officers are notorious for being short on detail. Police departments are getting younger all the time, but some of the bad old ideas are alive and well. You'll probably hear the phrase, sooner than later, "keep it short and sweet." This phrase should be etched in stone since older, experienced officers have been saying this to new officers for decades. They're referring to your written reports and probable cause statements. Many officers believe there is some inherent disadvantage in describing an incident in as much detail as possible. Nothing could be further from the truth.

…clear and concise detail

The whole reason for your being is to police society. It's not an easy job to catch bad people, but once you do, you have to lay the ground for keeping those bad people out of society for as long as possible. Short and sweet won't get it. You must describe the events of an incident in clear and concise detail. Police usually compare concise to short, but concise for you simply means your reporting should be free from embellishment. Word processing gives you the ability to present a description of events so that anyone reading it can feel they're actually witnessing those events.

…create and maintain

Sadly, most police departments are far from utilizing the vast investigative potential of computers. The incredible databases you see being used in movies, and by television cops and government agents, are as fictional as the shows themselves. The technology is real, and those databases, and many more, could exist if people in law enforcement knew how to create and maintain them. The keyword here is maintain. Creating an investigative database is not that difficult, but maintaining an investigative database is beyond the abilities of most departments.

…continuity and institutional memory

Youth and inexperience has displaced continuity and institutional memory. Command and supervisory levels mirror the youth of a department's police officers more than ever before. Computers could be a most desirable solution to reestablishing continuity and storing information lost with the departure of experienced police officers during the past decade. Unfortunately, youthful police officers, and their youthful leaders, will never have a terribly deep appreciation for continuity and institutional memory; until, they're no longer youthful.

…realize this correlation

Continuity is simply a continuous way of doing things. Your department's institutional memory is simply the aggregate knowledge gained through the experience of all its past and current members. As technology goes, the total logic of a computer program is perfectly compatible with continuity and institutional memory. If you're lucky, and the leaders of your department realize this correlation, you might experience the absolutely fabulous capabilities of well maintained investigative databases.

…confusion and chaos

No effective computer database, investigative or otherwise, can exist without the commitment to continuity. You'll undoubtedly hear the phrase, "thinking out of the box." If your department's leadership prides itself on thinking out of the box, and the leadership encourages subordinates to think out of the box, you'll find yourself working in an environment of confusion and chaos. You can think out of the box all you want as long as that thinking doesn't replace the organizational continuity contained inside the box.

…most important component

You, the individual police officer, are the most important component in the maintenance of an investigative database. The information you collect, on a daily basis, is far more valuable than you could ever believe. *If* your department has an efficient system to collect and enter information into an investigative database, the accuracy and completeness of the information you submit is all important. Police officers have a nasty habit of omitting information from a form, or report, they view as being irrelevant or unimportant. When omitted information is part of a database, the loss is critical.

…logic and application

With as far as computer technology has advanced, don't get your hopes up. The leadership of most departments are legends in their own minds. Most have plenty of experience in the politics of career advancement with little to no experience in the logic and application of information technology. The Holy Grail for police chiefs, and politicians, is the reduction of crime, and the proliferation of modern computer information technology has exceeded their wildest reduction expectations.

…unrelenting logic

You've certainly heard the phrase, "garbage in, garbage out." The unrelenting logic of computers requires a rigid level of quality control. Prior to desktops; laptops, and mobile reporting, hand written reports of crime were entered into a department's computer system at a centralized location where data entry was limited to a finite number of people. The responsibility for accurate data entry rested with a few, and quality control could be applied at a very high level.

…data entry error rates

Today, departments boast about direct data entry from the field, and the enormous savings realized in time and manpower. What they don't boast about are the difficulties associated with a lot of people entering data directly into a computer system. Because computers are so unrelentingly logical, data entry error rates are directly proportionate to the number of people entering data. For example, when a department goes from 10 people entering crime reporting data to 1,000 people entering the same data, one should be able to see the certain potential for problems.

…down is good

Everyone loves success no matter what kind of business they're in. In private industry, a computer system riddled with data errors would not be considered conducive to success. Ironically, just the opposite is true for a police department.

The work product of a police department is shown in its effectiveness in reducing crime. It follows that the accuracy of a department's crime reporting system is the all important factor in determining the department's level of success. Whether in business or police work, data errors will always impact negatively on the work product. In business, down is bad. In police work, down is good. In other words, the more errors made in reporting, and classifying, crime will result in a reduction of crime.

…would not be surprising

It may just be coincidental that the youthful transition of today's police departments, combined with the introduction of hi-tech information systems, is occurring alongside an historical reduction in violent crime across the nation. On the other hand, if one believes that departments are losing continuity and institutional memory, further complicated by inadequately maintained information systems, the same reduction in violent crime would not be surprising.

…least susceptible

There are only two violent crimes which are least susceptible to being ignored, under reported, purposely mis-classified, or mis-classified through data entry errors. The severity of the first, the importance of the second, and the relatively low number of both compared to all other violent crimes, makes them a good measure in assessing the validity of a department's violent crime reporting accuracy. It's not uncommon for a department to report a huge decrease in violent crime while showing only a negligible decrease in *homicides* and an increase in *bank robberies*. In fact, homicides and bank robberies will rarely show significant decreases from year to year.

…accuracy and completeness

As a brand new police officer, you must understand one thing. Information is what it is. You'll be collecting and transmitting information on a daily basis, and the way you collect and transmit that information will determine its value. If you're entering information directly into a computer system, you must adhere to two unwavering commitments…accuracy and completeness.

11

The Court Room

...a lot of time

You're going to spend a lot of time in the court room. As a new officer, this is not going to be a fun time, because you'll be making some stupid mistakes, and you'll be experiencing a lot of embarrassment. With the exception of lying, judges and prosecutors are pretty forgiving toward new, inexperienced officers.

...no less than a King or Queen

In the beginning, it's a good idea to spend some of your own time sitting in the court room and observing the proceedings. The most interesting, and informing, aspect of such observations is the judge. In the court room, the judge is no less that a King or Queen possessing absolute power. You'll quickly learn what pushes the judge's buttons. Some judges will impress you with their decorum, and competence, while others will come across as being no less than strange. Some will be very opinionated and quick to express those opinions. Others will shout, threaten, make jokes, or generally act like fools.

...most solemn environment

The one thing you always want to avoid is having a judge angry with you. Always go into a court room believing you're entering the most solemn environment on earth, because you are. The judge can act any way he or she wants...you can't. There is irony here. Outside the court room, a judge is subject to your authority no less than any other citizen, but inside the court room, you belong to the judge. If a judge calls you an idiot, you're an idiot. If the judge calls you stupid, you're stupid. Get the idea?

...completely truthful

The best way for you to make a good impression on any judge is to be truthful, and I mean completely truthful. If a judge even suspects you of lying, that judge will remember you. Thereafter, any testimony you give, before that judge, will be suspect, and your presence in that court room will be useless.

...no perfect case

Just as there is no perfect crime, you'll have no perfect case. During your court room observations, you may well watch an officer give perfect testimony in a case where the only evidence is the officer's credibility only to have the judge find the defendant not guilty. If the judge announces the verdict immediately following the officer's testimony, without even hearing the defendant's testimony, you can be certain the judge considers that officer to be a liar. You can also be certain that something occurred in the past which convinced the judge the officer is not credible.

...always tells the truth

Many years ago, I received a summons for a minor traffic case which had been lost in the system for well over two years. While I had a copy of the citation, I could not remember the defendant. I reasoned that when I saw the defendant in court, I would recognize him. On the day of trial, the defendant approached the defendant's table.

I had appeared before the sitting judge many times in the past. I stated to the judge, "Your Honor, I don't want to waste the court's time. I thought when I saw the defendant I would recognize him. Because of the long delay in this case, I simply don't remember this man." Before dismissing the charge against the defendant, the judge looked at the defendant and said, "The officer could have easily bluffed his way through this case, but Officer Baker always tells the truth." As I thought back on the many cases I'd had before that judge, I realized that I'd never lost a case before him. I've never forgotten that judge's assessment of my credibility, because, to me, it was the best compliment I've ever received.

...the only evidence

You'll appear in court many times with your word as the only evidence. If you read this entire book, and you learn only one thing, make the importance of your credibility that one thing. You will come under pressure many times to, let's say, embellish things. Don't ever do it! Your word belongs to you and you alone. If you're caught in a lie, no one will stand up and say, "Oh, I told the officer to say that."

...the truth will not be enough

Sometimes, although you do everything exactly right, the truth will not be enough. Imagine yourself on patrol in a high crime area, and you receive an anonymous call for a man armed with a gun. You receive an excellent physical description of the suspect, and when you arrive at the location, you see the suspect walking on the sidewalk. When the suspect sees you, he walks into a vacant lot where you lose sight of him. As you approach the lot, the suspect walks back out onto the sidewalk where you stop him. Surprise, surprise, your suspect has no gun.

Even though you're a brand new officer, you know the suspect dumped his gun in the vacant lot. When your back-up officer arrives, you walk into the lot, and you see a handgun laying on top of a pile of trash. As you leave the lot, you walk up to an elderly man who is sitting on his steps directly across from the lot. You ask the elderly gentleman, "Did you see this fellow throw this gun? The old man replies, "Sure, I saw him. He dropped that gun right where you picked it up."

When you walk back to the other officer, the officer takes you aside and asks, "Why were you talking to him?" You reply, "He's a witness. He saw the guy drop the gun." The officer then states, "He won't show up for court. You know this guy had the gun. You just say you saw him drop it. You'll lose the case if you don't say you saw him with it."

You go to court. The gun is stolen with no identifiable fingerprints. You have no other physical evidence. Just like the other officer said, your witness doesn't show for court. Without the witness, you lose the case.

...the judge knows

The judge is no idiot. The judge knows your defendant had the gun, and the judge knows you could have very easily said you saw your defendant drop the gun. Most importantly, the judge has identified you as an officer who does not take the value of your credibility lightly. Once you've established your credibility with the judges before whom you appear, you will never lose a case where the difference between conviction and acquittal rests solely on your credibility.

...no definitive definition of a jury

Most of your cases will be heard by a judge, in a court trial, where no jury is present. However, you will have occasions when you'll be testifying in front of a jury. Most juries consist of twelve persons; some jurisdictions employ a six juror panel. Beyond the number of people in a jury, there is no definitive definition of a jury. Jurors are typically chosen from voter roles which will make you more cognizant to the fragility of democracy.

...a whole different level

If you think some of the judges have a weird take on things, you'll soon learn that juries often operate on a whole different level. There will be times when you hear a verdict, and you'll wonder if you've entered the right court room. As a police officer, you may be called for jury duty, but it's unlikely you'll ever see the inside of a jury room. Since you'll never be privy to a jury's deliberations, it's not a bad idea to talk to one or more jurors after the verdict is announced, and the jury is dismissed by the judge.

The best juror to approach is usually the jury foreman. My experience has been that the jury's foreman is usually eager to answer your questions. Be prepared though, for he or she may express some very strange reasoning to you. No matter how silly that reasoning may sound, you have to remember that the purpose of the conversation is for you to listen and learn...not argue. If you're lucky, the judge will be part of the conversation. The fun part of having the judge participate is the possibility that the judge may explain to the juror, or jurors, why the verdict was off the wall.

I once had an armed home invasion with two victims and two defendants. I apprehended one of the suspects shortly after the crime, and I identified the second suspect. I obtained a search warrant for the first suspect's home where I recovered the suspects' weapons, and the property taken from the victims. The victims testified to all the events, and they positively identified both suspects. The crime scene, and overwhelming physical evidence, corroborated the victims' testimony. It was one of those cases where everything just fell into place. The jury deliberated for over three hours before returning with the verdicts.

The verdicts were strange to say the least. In this particular instance, the jury foreman approached the judge immediately following the trial. I took the opportunity to join the conversation. While both victims had the same crimes committed against them, the jury foreman explained that since the second victim did not live at the location, the jury found the defendants not guilty of robbing the second victim. There were some other strange anomalies which escape memory. At one point the foreman asked the judge, "What do you think, Your Honor?" The Judge, still seated behind the bench, drew a deep breath and sighed, "The evidence in this case was overwhelming. It should have taken you no more than fifteen minutes to find these defendants guilty on all counts." The Judge went on to explain that a jury has to determine only two things from the evidence presented. Did the crime occur, and did the defendant(s) commit the crime? He went on to muse about how jurors become lawyers as soon as they begin deliberation.

...avoid jury trials

The jury system is a wonderful thing more often for the guilty than for the innocent. The best way for you to avoid jury trials is through your case preparation. Too many officers overlook too many things. Every one of your cases, no matter how minor in nature, is important. If you get into the habit of doing a thorough investigation, and, more importantly, thoroughly documenting your investigation, few defense attorneys will try the case before a judge let alone a jury. When you've already answered all the defense attorney's questions in your documentation, the defendant's counsel will opt for a plea bargain nearly every time.

...aren't that bad

There's always some segment of the criminal justice system being criticized. Plea bargaining comes under the gun, from time to time, as a tool for simply unclogging the system. The simple truth is that there would be no functioning criminal justice system without plea bargaining. In any metropolitan area, where crime is a significant reality, plea bargains are more frequent than in jurisdictions with very low crime. Numbers do make a difference when time and financial resources are static items.

Criticism of plea bargains always emerges when the sentence derived from a particular plea bargain is ridiculously light in comparison with the seriousness of the crime. In most cases, where this situation exists, it's just a choice between conviction or dismissal. The reason for this choice almost always lies in the quality of the case. This is where you come in. If it's your case, and it's inadequate, then, you're just lucky to get the conviction.

Generally, plea bargains aren't that bad. You'll find the better your cases are the more frequently your cases will be plea bargained. On a good case, the sentence the defendant receives will be little less, or equal to, what he or she would receive in a court trial [judge]. In the event of a jury trial…well, who knows? Obtaining an adequate and certain sentence from a plea bargain is always preferable to throwing the dice on a jury trial.

…never appreciate the advantage

Next to the street, the court room will be your best educational source. Some police officers never appreciate the advantage of their experiences in the court room. You'll see the same officers repeatedly make the same mistakes, and those officers will criticize the court, the prosecutor, anybody or anything but themselves.

12

The Prosecutor

…do the heavy lifting

Contrary to what a lot of people believe, your primary duty is law *enforcement*. When you enforce laws, you end up arresting people. Every time you make an arrest, you begin a process culminating in the prosecution of that arrest. That's where the prosecutor comes into the picture. The prosecutor is the individual who will represent the state based on the testimony, and any other evidence, provided by you. The most often used titles for the chief prosecutor of a locality is District Attorney or State's Attorney. These elected officials employ assistants referred to as ADA's or ASA's. These assistants are the attorneys who do the heavy lifting prosecuting the cases for the state.

…difficulties faced by prosecutors

You're going to work with some very good prosecutors while others will leave you wondering if they attended an accredited law school. You'll have the ability to make a good prosecutor look outstanding, and a poor one look good. However, the ability and skill of the prosecutor isn't going to count for much if you don't deliver him or her a well prepared case. So many police officers fail to comprehend the difficulties faced by prosecutors. By far, the biggest problem for a prosecutor is time. Individual police officers often forget that his or her case is not the only case begin prosecuted. The ADA or ASA must review your case prior to trial, and the fewer questions you leave unanswered will make everyone's life a lot easier.

…sufficient to arrest

The first thing a prosecutor is going to see is your statement of probable cause. Probable cause is simply the reason(s) why you arrested the person being charged, and the charge(s) will be based on the probable cause you communicate. Probable cause confuses a lot of people, and police officers are often among the confused. Probable cause only has to be sufficient to arrest and charge a person; it need not be sufficient to convict a person of the crime alleged.

...serve everyone well

Most police officers seize on the "sufficient to arrest" part of probable cause to keep their probable cause statements "short and sweet." Some officers may, or may not, include more details in their police report. Many officers take the attitude that if the prosecutor wants more information, he or she can get a copy of the police report. A few officers will realize that a detailed probable cause statement will serve everyone well.

...one stop reference

While some of your cases will be complicated and require follow-up investigation, and reporting, most of your cases will be completed following arrest, and the initial reporting. In the latter situation, your probable cause statement can be a one stop reference for you, the prosecutor, and the defense attorney.

...anticipate any questions

Defense attorneys love to see brief probable cause statements. You'll make a defense attorney ecstatic if your police report contains only little more detail. When you write your probable cause statement, you should concentrate on accomplishing two things. First, you want to present an easily comprehended narrative of events from A to Z. Secondly, you should anticipate any questions a reasonable person might ask regarding the events, and you answer those questions in your narrative.

...loath to cross examine

If you subscribe to the "short and sweet" way of doing things, you're going to leave your prosecutor working in the dark. The defense attorney will view you less than competent, and a perfect candidate for cross examination. When a defense attorney sees a well written and comprehensive probable cause statement, that defense attorney will be hesitant to cross examine you. When the defense attorney sees all, or most, of his or her questions already addressed in your statement, the defense attorney will be loath to cross examine you.

…the prosecutor alone

Even today, some officers see an inherent disadvantage in providing detailed information in any of their reporting. These officers walk the fine line of withholding exculpatory information. Generally, a prosecutor must provide a defendant with all information revealed in your investigation, particularly, if the information is beneficial to the defendant's defense. In the rare instances where information is withheld from the defense, that decision always belongs to the prosecutor and the prosecutor alone. First, the prosecutor must have the information. You will never, never have any justification for withholding information from the prosecutor.

…small details

Everybody wants to win, and prosecutors are just as competitive as anyone else. Once you become experienced, you'll be able to provide your prosecutors with very well prepared cases. The small details will be second nature to you, and you'll leave few bases uncovered. It's a different matter in the beginning. You're going to miss some of those small details, and a missed small detail can be a headache for the prosecutor. While a prosecutor will never tell you to lie, you could find yourself listening to the question, "Are you sure you didn't do that?" The tone of that question could communicate to you the prosecutor's willingness to accept a harmless little lie. Ironically, if you fall for that one, your word will forever after be suspect with that prosecutor.

…excellent professional relationships

You're going to work with officers who never learn from their mistakes. When it comes to case preparation, those officers are going to make the same mistakes over and over. Of course, to them, it's always the prosecutor who is lazy, incompetent, or just doesn't know what he or she is doing. Prosecutors hate these guys, and it usually shows. As long as you protect your integrity, learn from your mistakes, and provide well prepared cases, you'll enjoy excellent professional relationships with your prosecutors.

13

Sergeants...
The Good, The Bad, The
Incompetent

...the good sergeant

Hopefully, you'll begin your career in a squad supervised by a good sergeant. In the beginning, you'll frequently find yourself in over your head on any number of occasions. A good sergeant will always be able to guide you through difficulties without subjecting you to embarrassment or ridicule. A good sergeant will be administratively strong, and he or she will have depth of experience in all types of situations encountered by a patrol officer. The good sergeant will always give you the credit for your good work realizing that your accomplishments reflect well on the sergeant and the squad. When you screw up, the good sergeant will be quick to intercede, and the sergeant will limit the damage protecting you from yourself.

The good sergeant realizes that the police officer is the single most important resource of the department. With this realization comes the second realization that the sergeant is a police officer's first, and best, shield from the tyranny of management. A good sergeant knows that one of the most difficult functions for a sergeant is balancing his or her loyalty between management and subordinates. This sergeant knows the importance of loyalty in both directions, and the good sergeant will diminish conflicts in loyalty by demanding that subordinates always act in good faith. Right or wrong, as long as you act in good faith, the good sergeant will never abandon you.

...the bad sergeant

On the other hand, you could begin by working for a bad sergeant. This type of sergeant will be strong in some areas; weak in most areas, and just plain wrong too much of the time. The bad sergeant will be narcissistic and self serving. The bad sergeant will be quick to take credit for things you do well. When you do something wrong, even at the direction of the bad sergeant, you'll be on your own. The bad sergeant will not only deny giving you bad direction, the bad sergeant will do everything in his or her power to ensure that you bear the entire responsibility for your incorrect action.

The bad sergeant is usually quick to make a decision. The relevancy of the decision being right or wrong is not usually that important to the bad sergeant. If you're the officer charged with implementing the decision, you could have a problem. If you refuse to follow the direction given by the sergeant, you could face a charge of insubordination. The bad sergeant will compound the problem for you. While the bad sergeant will have a reputation for faulty decision making, the bad sergeant will rarely, if ever, explain the reasoning for his or her decision. Here's your dilemma, and this is the reason why it's so important for you to learn as much as you can as fast as you can. Remember, any order given to you by any supervisor must be a lawful order. Just because an order does not sit well with your view of the world does not mean it's unlawful. However, if you know the order to be illegal, or in contravention to your department's rules, regulations, or procedures, it is your duty to make the sergeant aware of the contradiction, and your refusal to implement the order.

As a new officer, the bad sergeant will not have much, if any, respect for your point of view on any matter. If you question an order, or direction, from the bad sergeant, always do it in private. Never question the sergeant in the presence of other police officers or the public. If you do so in front of others, and you're wrong, the bad sergeant will humiliate you. If you do so in front of others, and you're right, you've made an enemy for life.

The bad sergeant will run a squad comprised of three distinct groups of subordinates. The foremost group will be those loyal to the sergeant. The second group will be those considered to be disloyal, and the third group will be the independents. Intrigue is an important component to the bad sergeant's method of supervision. While a good sergeant deplores rumors and personality conflicts, the bad sergeant encourages turmoil among members of the squad. The bad sergeant, through rumor and innuendo, will use the loyal members to help him or her control the disloyal. At first glance, you might think you'd be better off being a member of the loyal group; however, being a member of the loyal group means conforming to the bad sergeant's thinking, and methods, in every way, shape, and form. Of course, it's not a question of simply joining one of the groups. The sergeant will determine your group membership status in the squad.

The bad sergeant's definition of disloyalty can be very broad. A simple disagreement with the sergeant can land you in the disloyal group. You don't want to be a member of this group. The disloyal group always provides the one officer who occupies the very bottom of the food chain. This is a position that exists in every squad, and it's not unique to the bad sergeant's squad. Even in a good sergeant's squad, there will be one officer who receives an abundance of abuse, and criticism, from the other squad members. It's usually a rotating position brought upon an officer by his or her own doing. Unless the officer is a total loser, he or she will eventually rotate out to make room for the next offender. The good sergeant will make every effort to help the officer rehabilitate; whereas, the bad sergeant has no interest in rehabilitation, and the bad sergeant will choose the officer who will occupy this position. If you're the chosen one, your only reprieve will come when another member of the disloyal group offends the bad sergeant more than you.

The independent group will be the smallest group. When I say small, I mean small. In fact, it might not be a group at all. If you're an independent, you could find yourself all alone. If you are alone, it's not a bad thing. The bad sergeant will do everything in his or her power to limit the number of officers in this group since this group is comprised of officers the bad sergeant views as not susceptible to negative influence. When working for a bad sergeant, the independent status is your best bet. You can be assured of membership in the independent group if the bad sergeant views you as a person possessing dangerously high integrity, knowledge, and self confidence. While the sergeant, and members of the loyal group, will distrust you, they'll be careful not to include you in any unethical or compromising situations. The so called disloyal group will respect, and envy, your independence.

…the incompetent sergeant

You could do worse than the incompetent sergeant. As long as you have good reasoning power, and a healthy amount of paranoia, you'll be able to co-exist with this type of sergeant, and make it on your own. The incompetent sergeant will rarely be of any help to you, but this sergeant will rarely do anything to hurt you. When faced with a decision making event, this sergeant will always choose the path of least resistance, or he or she will waffle until someone else implements a course of action. As long as you're a quick learner, and you make sound decisions, you'll probably do well working for this sergeant.

The incompetent sergeant will often possess a pleasant personality, and he or she will consistently avoid confrontation with members of his or her squad or other supervisors. This sergeant will rarely refuse requests from squad members, such as requests for irregular days off, even if those requests adversely affect the efficient operation of the squad. Some members of your squad, and other supervisors, will regularly take advantage of the incompetent sergeant at the expense of you and your fellow squad members. The same people who regularly exploit this sergeant's incompetence will be the first to criticize, and ridicule, the incompetent sergeant behind his or her back.

…lucky enough

No matter what kind of sergeant you draw, your goal, from the outset, should be to make yourself self sufficient. If you're lucky enough to start off with a good sergeant, make good use of that time to develop your skills. You're not going to have that good sergeant indefinitely, and you have to prepare yourself for the other two. You will, at some point, work for the bad and the incompetent.

14

Supervisor's Complaint

…the type of complaint

Your department will have its own criteria for handling complaints made by citizens against police officers. When a citizen makes a complaint against you, it will most frequently go directly to your immediate supervisor. Depending upon the type of complaint, and the procedures of your department, your supervisor will determine if the complaint can be resolved by the supervisor.

…misunderstandings

Some complaints may be of a nature serious enough to require the supervisor to investigate and submit a written report to your Internal Affairs Division. However, the vast majority of supervisors' complaints deal with misunderstandings between officers and citizens.

…useless advice

Right from the beginning, you'll hear other officers, and some supervisors alike, make the following statement, "If you don't get complaints, you're not doing your job." When you hear this comment, file it away with all the other useless advice you're going to receive.

…really strange people

As a new officer, you can pick up bad habits really fast. One of the worst is an inability to converse with people you consider to be not worth your time. When a person seeks your assistance, you should keep in mind that the person who called you thinks his or her problem is serious enough to call police. To be sure, you're going to run into some really strange people, and many of those people are going to be so irritating. Some situations will be funny while others will be simply ridiculous, but, funny or ridiculous, to those people they're not.

…attitude

As a police officer, it's not your job to laugh at, or ridicule, any person just because that person's sense of proportion does not fit your view of normality. The vast majority of supervisors' complaints will reveal no wrongdoing by the officers. What they will reveal is the complainants' displeasure with the officers' attitudes. You have to remember that every person, regardless of his or her station in life, can be insulted.

…sympathetic listener

Even if there's nothing you can do to help the person, it doesn't take that much time to make the person believe you at least care about his or her plight. Frequently, a sympathetic listener is all the person really wants. Who knows, there might come a time when you're in a really bad situation, and one of those silly people is the only person nearby to call 911 and get you some help. You may say the odds are against that…not as much as you'd think.

…order of the day

If you're working for a good squad supervisor, which is normally a sergeant, that sergeant will not be wasting his or her time resolving needless supervisor's complaints. If you land in a squad where such complaints are the order of the day, be careful, you're on your own. If a sergeant cannot control the behavior of his or her subordinates, that sergeant will be weak in other areas as well.

…enough is never enough

No matter how much you try to placate people, you will generate a supervisor's complaint at some point. Sometimes, enough is never enough. If you give the situation your best effort, your supervisor will experience the same frustration when interviewing the complaining person. More importantly, your lack of supervisor's complaints will identify you as a self sufficient officer requiring minimal supervision.

15

Internal Investigations

...transparency of IAD investigations

Everyone who watches the cop shows on television should be familiar with the Internal Affairs Division or IAD. The name may vary among departments, but it's all the same. The IAD is a unit within a police department charged with investigating complaints of wrong doing against police officers. The transparency of IAD investigations depend upon state and local laws. There are confidential aspects to any ongoing police investigation; however, the secrecy involved in an IAD investigation can be extreme.

...absence of checks and balances

At first glance, you might think secrecy would be to your benefit. Indeed, your benefit is always the reason given when a department seeks extra secrecy protection when conducting internal investigations. Secrecy is supposed to protect you against false allegations, and false allegations against police officers are quite common. The problem with any secretive organization is the absence of checks and balances where corruption, and political influence, can flourish. Television dramas and movies aren't normally a good reference for real police procedures; however, their usually negative depictions of internal investigation units are pretty accurate.

...confuse and befuddle

Police officers are the strangest creatures. One would think that a police officer would be one of the most difficult people to interrogate. In fact, just the opposite is true. Even the most inept IAD investigator can very often confuse and befuddle the most experienced police officer.

There are four occasions when you'll come into contact with your IAD:

1. You're a suspect in an investigation of criminal activity.

2. You're a suspect in an investigation of a serious violation of departmental rules, regulations, or procedures.

3. You may be a witness to a criminal or departmental violation allegedly committed by another police officer(s).

Or,

4. You've incurred the wrath of a politician, a politically influential anybody; a co-worker, a vengeful spouse, or just about anyone who knows there'll be no cost to him or her for making your life difficult.

…number 4

The majority of your department's IAD resources will be occupied with number 4. Most of the investigations will be frivolous, and they could be resolved quickly. However, rarely is any IAD investigation resolved quickly. IAD investigations are slow and cumbersome for one main reason. Where a desired outcome cannot be obtained, or the desired outcome doesn't even exist, the investigation will probably never be officially closed. The perpetual open status of an investigation will ensure its secrecy, and you will never have the opportunity to fully understand the scope, and real purpose, of the investigation against you.

…exercise every right available to you

Needless to say, you never want to have any involvement with an IAD investigation, but it's likely you'll have involvement at some point. Make yourself familiar with your department's procedures for internal investigations. If you become a target of an internal investigation, always…did I say *always*?…exercise every right available to you. In every instance where you're entitled to have legal counsel present, you're just stupid if you don't exercise that right. When giving a statement to IAD with your legal counsel present, the IAD investigator is going to be on his or her best behavior. However, if you go into an IAD interview accompanied only by your innocence, you're a fool.

…corrupt investigative practices

If you ever find yourself the subject of a serious complaint requiring representation by legal counsel, you've obviously got a problem. Some police officers, even experienced ones, often think their innocence displaces the need to retain legal counsel. They even think, that by retaining an attorney, they're inferring guilt where there is none. This is a naive view to which you should never subscribe. Look at it this way. If you're innocent, and you need an attorney, somebody is out to do you. Forget about fairness, it just doesn't exist in an internal investigation. As a police officer, you have no advocacy to rise in your defense to prevent tainted or corrupt investigative practices.

…legal counsel

If you do find yourself in need of legal counsel, you'll probably have one of three options. First, your department will furnish legal counsel. Second, if you're a member of a fraternal or labor organization, that organization may provide an attorney. Third, you shop for a lawyer out of your own pocket.

…less than zealous

If you take the first option for retaining legal counsel, you're either brain damaged or just naturally stupid. The second option is the one most often used by police officers. However, a fraternal or labor organization can only exist through co-existence with the department, and the government the department serves. If the complaint against you comes from an influential person(s) from within the government, the department, or your own organization, the legal representation you receive could be less than zealous. By far, the third option will be most advantageous to you. Every town or city has a reputable and competent attorney who is familiar with its police department's conduct, or misconduct, of internal investigations, and the nuances of the department's administrative procedures. It's really no different than anything else…you get what you pay for.

…witness statement

IAD investigators live and breathe on audio tape, so, in nearly all instances, you're going to be interviewed on tape. If you're summoned to give a taped witness statement, you won't be entitled to legal counsel. You may not even know the subject to be discussed; until, the interview begins. At the beginning of the taped interview, the investigator should state, on the record, that you are not a suspect in the investigation, nor is there any view toward charging you with a criminal or departmental offense.

…just say, "No"

Never have an *off the record* conversation with an IAD investigator before, or during, the taped interview. If you respond for a witness statement, and the investigator asks you, "Can we talk off the record," just say, "No." When this question is asked, the investigator is telling you he or she is not prepared, or you are suspected of something. It will probably be a combination of both. Without a doubt, your refusal to talk off the record will raise all kinds of red flags with the investigator, but so what?

…no need for off the record conversation

As a new officer, and an innocent one at that, don't believe for one second that an IAD investigator is your friend. Your refusal to talk off the record will not set a good tone for the interview, but again, so what?" If the investigator continues to engage you off the record, simply tell the investigator you'll answer all of his or her questions on the record. If you're there simply to give a witness statement, there should be no need for off the record conversation. If the investigator is going to take a taped statement, he or she should already know you have pertinent information, and the investigator should already have the pertinent questions formulated.

…verbal abuse and threats

During the taped interview, the investigator might stop the tape for the purpose of clarifying an issue, or you could find yourself being the subject of verbal abuse and threats during this intermission. Either way, don't respond to anything. When the taping resumes, make reference to any off the record comments made by the investigator. If you were the subject of abusive language, repeat those comments in the exact words used by the investigator. I can safely guarantee that you'll be unable to get much of it on the record. You'll be amazed how fast the investigator's finger will find the off button. It will also be the end of the interview. When, or if, you're summoned to come back for the interview, it will be conducted by a different investigator with no desire for off the record conversation.

…a bad cop

On occasion, an IAD investigation may actually build a relatively strong case against a bad cop. When a police officer engages in criminal activity, or commits serious violations of departmental regulations, one can safely assume that lying is also part of that officer's resume. Self preservation dictates that such an officer will try to save his or her job, or stay out of jail, by giving investigators something better than what they've already got. Deals are made all the time in the course of normal criminal investigations with normal criminals, but criminal police officers are not normal criminals.

…worse than themselves

One of the worst IAD practices is treating a bad cop as if he or she were some street corner junkie caught with a bag of dope. Unfortunately, an IAD can, too often, be duped by bad cops into believing that they can deliver officers worse than themselves. As your career progresses, you'll soon identify those officers who you know to be unfit. They'll seem immune to investigation while others working around them are frequently under investigation for any number of different violations. When you encounter such an officer, disassociate yourself from that officer as much as possible. At some point, that officer will go down over something even his or her IAD handlers can't condone or ignore.

…predetermined outcome

Relative to the number of complaints/cases an IAD investigates, you'll rarely see IAD investigations result in criminal prosecutions of police officers. When criminal prosecutions do occur, most will reveal poor investigations and case preparations. Some may even reveal actions by IAD investigators that are more reprehensible than the alleged criminal conduct of the officer being tried. Poor IAD investigations are a result of inexperienced investigators, incompetent investigators, and investigations designed to conform to predetermined outcomes.

…lower standard

A department's IAD exists to function at a much lower standard than the department's real detectives who have to produce quality investigations and adhere to rules of evidence. The IAD is a purely political entity, masquerading as an investigative unit, designed to serve a department's political interests in the finest traditions of cronyism and political correctness.

…politics and personal relationships

Regardless of the size of a department, politics and personal relationships bare too heavily on the conduct and outcome of internal investigations. Police chiefs across the nation will continue to state what a great job they're doing policing their departments; just don't believe it.

16

Sexual Harassment

...career ending transgressions

You'll soon learn there are a number of career ending transgressions you can commit, and sexual harassment is one of them. Unless your department is operating in a vacuum, it's going to have a detailed written directive on the subject. During your quest for knowledge in the first few months, put this one near the top of your list. As a new officer with no authority over fellow officers, you're at lower risk than a supervisor. However, while you're on your probationary period, you can be fired for just about anything. Don't let something as preventable as sexual harassment end your career, before it gets started.

...political correctness

Every definition, and interpretation, of sexual harassment purports equal applicability to both genders. Smirk...smirk. This is one of those polite fictions which must exist to make the enforcement of sexual harassment laws possible. In reality, as a male officer, you are much more vulnerable to your department's sexual harassment policy than if you're a female officer. While a sexual harassment complaint against you as a female officer will be entertained, you don't have as much to worry about. Investigators will feel pressure to produce evidence to exonerate you; whereas, if you're a male, the pressure will be to produce evidence to sustain the complaint against you. This condition is simply a cultural bias reinforced by an environment of political correctness.

...positions of authority

Okay...so, everybody knows that sexual harassment laws and policies were never created with the protection of men in mind. You, as a female police officer, should not take much comfort in this fact. Police departments are hiring female officers in increasing numbers, and females are occupying positions of authority more than ever before. As this trend continues, the inherent bias of sexual harassment enforcement will become more and more difficult to justify.

…ruin everybody's day

As generally understood, sexual harassment does exist. The hostile work environment definition has made just about every interaction between males and females subject to an interpretation of sexual harassment. Officers of the same sex can make derogatory comments to one another, and those comments are simply considered rude. When those same comments are made between the sexes, they can ruin everybody's day.

…the worst enemy

In every aspect of a police officer's job, the worst enemy you'll have is your own mouth. The things you say, and the way you say them, will either get you into trouble or keep you out of trouble. Making comments of a sexual nature is the best way to start yourself on the road to a lot of aggravation. If you're smart, you'll leave the sexual innuendos away from the job…far, far away from the job.

…a few methods

If you believe you've become a victim of sexual harassment, there are a few methods you have available to resolve the situation:

1. You can tell the offending officer, in clear and concise language, to knock it off. You can deliver this message in private or in the presence of witnesses.

Too simple. Okay, lets try this one:

2. When in the presence of the offending officer, prepare yourself by anticipating the offending comments. When a comment is made, respond with a comment designed to belittle the nature of the offending comment. You should never respond with an argumentative or similar offending comment.

If the combination of 1 & 2 doesn't work, you're dealing with a real moron. Now, you have only two options left:

3. Continue with number 2, or go on to number 4.

4. Report the offending behavior to your supervisor.

…No

The problem with number 4 is that it's not as simple as it sounds. Before you go to number 4, read and *comprehend* your department's policy on sexual harassment complaints. In most instances, when an officer approaches his or her supervisor, the officer is initially looking for an informal solution. When you ask your supervisor, "Can we talk off the record," your supervisor's response should be, "No." The supervisor should explain to you that the matter you want to discuss could be one requiring formal reporting.

…Sure

Here's the other side of that coin. You could have a supervisor who isn't too keen on the official rule book. In this scenario, you ask your supervisor the same question, "Can we talk off the record?" Your supervisor responds, "Sure." You explain the actions of the offending officer, and you ask the supervisor to speak with the offending officer. Your supervisor agrees, and you go away thinking that will be the end of the matter. If this works, great, but you'll probably be disappointed when it doesn't work.

…every time it occurs

Here's the best way to deal with sexual harassment. Document what you believe to be sexual harassment each and every time it occurs. Write down the date; time; location; exact statement(s) made; description of physical contact if any; name(s) of any witness(es) present, and your request to the offending officer to cease his or her behavior. Continue with steps 1 and 2 until the behavior ceases, or you decide to continue to step 4.

…knowledgeable sergeant

If you're working for a knowledgeable sergeant who knows the importance of a well adjusted working environment, you won't have to worry about sexual harassment. This sergeant will take the appropriate action, on his or her own, at the first indication of any inappropriate behavior of one member toward another.

…a whole new level

Sexual harassment reaches a whole new level when a supervisor is accused of sexual harassment. Your department will take this accusation of harassment more seriously since this is where deep pockets are put into jeopardy.

…extremely serious

Sexual harassment by a supervisor, in any form, is an extremely serious situation for the subordinate being affected. A supervisor's influence over a new officer's career cannot be overstated. If you, as a new officer, become a victim of sexual harassment by a supervisor, you're going to feel pretty powerless.

…isn't too bright

You're not powerless. Any supervisor who harasses a subordinate for sexual favors, or just because the subordinate is the opposite sex, isn't too bright. Any supervisor, no matter how high in rank, can go down for being so stupid. Supervisors who engage in such activity usually don't have much appreciation for their department's policy regarding sexual harassment, and its applicability to them.

…potential nightmare

If I were a new officer being sexually harassed, along with my repeated requests of the supervisor to cease the harassment, I'd give the supervisor ample opportunity to provide me with enough instances of documented, and verifiable, harassment to make his or her life a potential nightmare. I'd then present a representative sample of my evidence to the supervisor. If the supervisor has a single active brain cell, he or she will avoid me like a disease.

…loath to file a complaint

In order to pursue a complaint of sexual harassment, you'll have to do so in accordance with your department's policy. I, personally, would be loath to file a complaint of sexual harassment. When you file a complaint of sexual harassment, it never ends well. Sexual harassment splits people into groups. You'll have your supporters, and the accused will have his or hers. Even if you prevail in a formal complaint of sexual harassment, you'll carry the label of accuser for a long time afterward.

17

Domestic Violence

…a lot of grief

There is no other identifiable group of persons on the planet more vulnerable to the consequences of domestic violence than American police officers. If you're involved in a domestic relationship with the potential to become violent, and you intend to remain in the relationship, do yourself a favor and don't waste your time becoming a police officer. Or, after you become a police officer, and you enter into such a relationship, you're stupid, and you should prepare yourself for a lot of grief beyond the crummy relationship.

…domestic dispute

Not that many years ago, domestic violence was not treated as it should have been. Police officers routinely talked to battling spouses, partners, etc., leaving the problem to the next shift. When a police officer was involved in a domestic dispute, the same routine was usually followed. When an officer's situation made it to a supervisory level, counseling was usually as far as it went.

…shocked….shocked

Like everything else that makes it into the world of political correctness, the total eradication of domestic violence is now the ultimate, impossible goal. The same people who view police officers as some of the most imperfect examples of humanity are shocked…shocked mine you when an allegation of domestic violence is leveled at a police officer. Because domestic violence has become such a politically charged issue, a police officer is the most effective target for zealots and politicians.

…mere allegation

You must keep in mind that a mere allegation of domestic violence against you, with absolutely no evidence to corroborate the allegation, can be enough to end your career. In an instance where an allegation is insufficient to take you into a court room, your department could still try you in an administrative proceeding. Despite the lack of evidence, your chances in such a proceeding are not good. If you're still on your probationary period, start looking for other employment. If you're terminated for domestic violence under any circumstance, your career in law enforcement is over.

…glaring exception

Both male and female police officers are subject to the same departmental treatment in matters of domestic violence. Well, theoretically anyway. In an age where women are considered equal to men in every respect, domestic violence is the glaring exception. Statistically, men are, overwhelmingly, the perpetrators of domestic violence, so why should it surprise anyone when female police officers are treated more benignly than male officers when accused of domestic violence?

…the weaker sex

Things aren't going to change anytime soon, because cultural bias still trumps political correctness in one respect, and most people, including police, still view the female as the weaker sex. The contradiction is stark. The same people who insist that female officers are equal to men, when confronting a predominantly male violent criminal culture, can't bring themselves to accept the possibility that those same female officers could be aggressors in their own domestic relationships. Except…if you're a female officer who is in a lesbian relationship, you'll find that an accusation of domestic violence against you will bring you parity with male officers relative to the greater risk associated with that parity.

…undoubtedly guilty

Domestic violence has always been against the law particularly since domestic violence incidents often result in some form of physical assault. In the past, had police officers, prosecutors, and courts treated domestic violence with the seriousness it deserved, police officers today probably would not be held to the standard of undoubtedly guilty until proven maybe innocent.

…pay a heavy price

Your jeopardy doesn't stop with your own domestic relationship. Most, if not all states, have enacted legislation on domestic violence. Your department will also have a written procedure for handling domestic violence incidents. If you deviate from the law, or your department's directive, in handling domestic violence incidents, you might as well go home and punch your own spouse, partner, etc., in the nose. If you're stupid enough to believe that you're in some way immune from adhering to domestic violence rules, you'll sooner or later pay a heavy price.

…that exception

The bad thing about a rule is that there is always that exception to the rule. Imagine yourself sitting in your patrol car taking care of some paper work just before the end of your shift. Out of the corner of your eye, you see a woman walking toward you. As she gets closer, you think to yourself how familiar she looks, but you can't place where you've seen or met her. The woman stops and leans forward at your open driver's door window. In a somewhat distraught, but firm, tone the woman says, "Officer, my husband just assaulted me."

Just as the woman finishes her short statement, your stomach makes one of those really uncomfortable twisting movements. You've just recalled why this woman is familiar; she's the wife of your police chief. Your first reaction is absolutely correct. You take a deep breath and silently say to yourself, "I'm screwed." To say you've experienced some bad luck would be a gross understatement, for no matter what action you take from this point on, your pain will probably be severe.

As bad as this situation is, you have no choice but to handle the incident exactly as you'd handle any other incident of domestic violence. It's going to get complicated since the police chief is involved. You're going to create a panic as soon as you notify your supervisor, and the panic will increase as your unwelcome notification rises through the department's chain of command. While you realize the incident should be reported and handled by departmental procedures, that decision will not be yours. For this reason, as soon as you've told yourself that you're screwed, you should be on your radio calling for your supervisor.

At the very instant that woman uttered the words, "My husband assaulted me," she established probable cause that a crime had been committed. The sooner she repeats that same allegation to your supervisor, the sooner some of the weight will be lifted from your shoulders. It's not inconceivable that you would be directed to handle this incident differently from established procedures. If you should receive such direction, you should refuse to depart from the established procedures. If you're lucky, your refusal will cause your supervisor to remove you from the investigation entirely.

...naive assumption

As much as you might like to think that rules apply to everyone equally, it's a naive assumption. While the assumption may be naive, your application of rules must never be influenced by who someone is or by what that someone's position may be. Doing things right may not always serve you well in the short term, as in the example above, but doing things right will always be to your benefit in the long term.

18

Emergency Response and Vehicle Pursuits

…some type of written directives

Isn't it exciting? You see it frequently on television. You see it from the dash camera of the police car or from the news helicopters. You will, at some point, be put in the position to pursue, or not pursue, a suspect vehicle. Nearly all police departments have some type of written directives detailing under what circumstances you may engage in a vehicle pursuit.

…good intentions

Unless you're a coward, or just lazy, the thought of letting a criminal escape from you is repugnant. The problem with being young, and new to policing, is the absence of experience, and the realization that your good intentions can place you in jeopardy beyond your imagination.

…the biggest weapon

The firearms you train with, and carry, are not the only deadly weapons you'll have in your possession. Your patrol car is the biggest weapon, and the one least under your control. Automobile accidents happen all the time, and police officers have more than their fair share.

…training and punishment

Every department in the nation is in a continuous struggle to find ways to reduce their fleet accident rate. No matter what new ideas are proposed, or implemented, they always take the form of training and punishment. It's difficult to measure the success of training and punishment standards since both vary from department to department. Training can be a combination of actual driving training and classroom instruction. The classroom instruction is going to cover liability issues as well as driver training. Punishment can range from slight to severe. Slight could be loss of pay for several days, and the suspension of your departmental driver's license. Severe could be termination of your employment.

…driving experience

You'll fall into one of two categories. Many new recruits will have little or no driving experience obtaining their drivers' licenses just prior to entering police training. The second category will be those who have driving experience with their driving habits, good or bad, set and resistant to change. If you develop good driving habits as a new driver, or you already have good habits as an experienced driver, you'll be off to a really good start.

…injured or even killed

Whether you're naturally cautious or reckless behind the wheel, police officers will inadvertently lend more peer support to a reckless driver over a cautious one. When you find yourself in a really bad situation and need help, you know that the reckless driver is going to violate every traffic law to reach you…if he or she makes it. Herein lies the rub. At some point, without exception, the reckless driver is not going to make it. None of the outcomes are good. The reckless driver is going to be injured or even killed, or the reckless driver is going to injure or kill someone else.

…effectiveness of sirens

As a new officer, you might believe that a siren is a magical device that parts the waters. Unfortunately, some officers never lose that belief. Even after years of experience, they're still cursing drivers who won't disappear into thin air. You can train yourself right now on the effectiveness of sirens. As you drive or ride in a vehicle, and you hear a siren, start taking mental notes.

First, identify the siren as coming from a police car, an ambulance, or a fire engine. Starting backward, the fire engine is easy. It's big, really loud, and relatively slow. You have sufficient time to determine its direction, and get out of its way. The ambulance is also bigger than a police car. Its siren is usually louder than a police car, and its speed is often slower than the fire engine. Again, you have time to see the ambulance, and get out of its way. The police car is a different thing all together. It's smaller, faster, and it's on top of you before you have time to react. In most cases, when you hear the siren, you won't know if the police car is setting on your bumper or about to pass in front of you.

...arrive at your destination

The ambulance is the best example to pattern your driving when running with your siren in built up areas or in moderate to heavy traffic. Your tires won't be squealing; smoke won't be pouring from your wheel wells, but your brakes will be there when you need them. Most importantly, you'll arrive at your destination, and you won't kill anyone in the process. Surprisingly, you'll find that if Officer Reckless does arrive before you, he or she was probably closer when the response began. Remember, you'll be traveling at a relatively constant speed giving drivers the time needed to yield to you. If you're driving like Officer Reckless, you're going to spend a lot of time stopping, starting, and startling people. You'll be placing yourself, and others, in peril for injury or worse.

...pursuit of a vehicle

At some point, you will have to decide on whether or not to engage yourself in the pursuit of a fleeing vehicle. When you engage in the pursuit of a vehicle, that decision lies entirely with you; until, you put the pursuit over your radio. At that point, the continuation of the pursuit is the responsibility of your supervisor or any supervisor for that matter.

...break it off

Some departments are more sensitive to vehicle pursuits than others. Safety is a concern, but liability is the overriding issue. While one supervisor may inquire as to the reason for the pursuit, another supervisor may tell you to break it off before learning any details. If you're told to break off the pursuit, you'd better do so. If you continue the pursuit, and it ends badly, no one...but no one...will share the responsibility with you.

...following a vehicle

Some officers consider themselves clever, and they'll transmit not a pursuit, but a following. If you're simply following a vehicle, that's fine. If you're in a pursuit, and you say you're just following, you're not going to fool anyone. Every time you transmit information over your radio, you're providing a record of your "following" that can be easily analyzed. The time between the locations you give will indicate your speed. Speed is the major determining factor between following and pursuing.

…no control of the vehicle you're pursuing

When you engage in a pursuit, you're going to have enough trouble controlling your own vehicle and concentrating on other important things. Your mind is going to be taking note of your locations, and you'll be transmitting your location as often as possible. Unlike the idiot you're chasing, you've got to avoid tunnel vision, and stay aware of the conditions around you. Even if you do everything perfectly, you have to understand that you have absolutely no control of the vehicle you're pursuing.

…make it clear

There is no definitive method to use when deciding to continue a vehicle pursuit. The authorization to continue a pursuit will be based primarily on the information provided by you. Never embellish that information. Transmit only factual information based on circumstances you observe, or, if second party information is relevant, make it clear to the supervisor authorizing the pursuit what information is secondhand.

…one horrible time

Whatever the outcome of a vehicle pursuit, there will be criticism. If the pursuit ends with serious injury or death, the criticism will be deafening. If you initiate a pursuit, and the worst happens, you'll be in for one horrible time. Witnesses will come out of the woodwork describing your reckless conduct of the pursuit. Some of the witness descriptions will be so outrageous you won't even recognize the described events as being even remotely related to your pursuit.

…use your head

As a police officer, you are duty bound to catch the bad guy; however, when the bad guy is trying to escape behind the wheel of a vehicle, there are two standards to which you must adhere. First, make yourself throughly familiar with your department's guidelines on vehicle pursuits, and follow those guidelines to the letter. Second, use your head, and don't get caught up in the excitement. Weigh the importance of apprehending your suspect against the possibility of injury to innocent people. The easiest way to figure this one is to ask yourself this question. Would you want a police officer to chase this guy if there was a possibility he might crash into a car occupied by members of your own family?

...terrible responsibility

Well, I never said this would be an easy one, and it never will be an easy decision to make. You've just got to remember that when you pursue a vehicle, you are taking on a terrible responsibility.

19

Use of Force

...sticks and stones

Unless you're a person who wants to be a police officer just to bully people under color of authority, you probably believe that a uniform, and the authority it conveys, will offer you some form of physical protection. Some is the operative word here. For some people, your authority will be enough. For more people than you'd like to consider right now, your authority will not be enough. Even with your bullet proof vest, sticks and stones...and bullets will still hurt you.

...choking you into unconsciousness

If you're a person who deplores the idea of using physical force, get another career. If you're a person who has the ability, willingness, and thoughtfulness to use force when necessary, you'll do alright when the time comes. Without any doubt, you'll be required to use force many times during your career. During your training, you'll be taught a theory called "escalation of force." All this means is that you employ only enough force to overcome the force against you. If the suspect is using only his hands to resist you, you use your hands. If you're unable to subdue the suspect with your hands, you may escalate to spraying the suspect with chemical pepper spray. If the suspect has you on the ground, and he is choking you into unconsciousness, you can, theoretically, shoot the suspect if that is the only method left to you.

...adrenaline...panic

Remember, adrenaline is your friend, and panic is your enemy. Never confuse the two. Adrenaline is a physical response to danger, and panic is a state of mind. Being a police officer does not make a person immune from panic; however, a police officer must be a person who realizes that panic serves no useful purpose. Think about it. Your body automatically aids you with increased adrenaline in the face of danger. While your body is wired and ready to go, your mind is still the controlling mechanism for directing that added strength. The presence of panic makes the advantage of adrenaline useless, and it could cost you your life.

…force with reason

You must be prepared to exercise force with reason. A police officer soon learns that reasonable people are rare. A police officer not only must decide a reasonable course of action, the officer must then, frequently, employ some degree of force to implement the action. Force can be problematic. Sometimes, a firm and resolute posture will do the trick. Other times, physical force will be required. In the absence of imminent physical threat, force should always be the last option. Attempts to reason with, even unreasonable, people should always be the first option.

…eye of the beholder

You're entering a career unlike any other. Everybody, no matter what their profession or occupation, knows how to do your job better than you. This is especially true where physical force is involved. The degree, and need, for physical force is always in the eye of the beholder. Whenever you're required to use force, no matter how minimal, there will almost always be some self styled expert nearby to judge your use of force as excessive. The expert layman's term for excessive force is police brutality. I can't think of a more overused term that, when alleged, will excite the media, activate politicians, and cause police executives to pledge new use of force procedures even before excessive force has been determined.

…easy example

Your only defense against an allegation of excessive force is the absence of excessive force. Let's look a an easy example: You respond to a call for a suspicious man. As soon as you approach the man, he takes a swing at you. His fist barely misses your face as you duck away from the punch. Remembering escalation of force, you draw your pepper spray canister from your belt, and you spray it at the suspect. Just your luck, it's a windy day, and you get a dose of the nasty stuff as well as your attacker. You don't know why the suspect attacked you, but now he's angrier than ever. He comes at you again, and both of you go down on the asphalt. Your stick falls out of its ring and goes rolling down the street as the two of you punch and kick each other.

Just when you're getting worried, you roll on top of him and land a good punch to the suspect's jaw. You know you've won the day when you see his eyes roll back, and he falls into semi-consciousness. You don't waste any time. You roll him over onto his stomach, and you get him securely handcuffed. By this time, help should be arriving. Even in the worst neighborhoods, there are a lot of people who are on your side. They don't want to see harm come to you, and they will call 911.

It's hard to tell which one of you got the worst of the battle. Both of you are bloodied and bruised. Your suspect looks a bit worse. His eye is beginning to swell shut from that lucky punch you landed. There's a crowd of people watching as the suspect is about to be taken away by one of the back up officers. The suspect calls to you asking if he can talk to you. He voices the request in a submissive tone, and you walk over to him. Well, he must have been saving this one. By the time you realize what's coming, it's too late, and a nasty glob of bloodied saliva hits you right in the face.

There's not too many things that are as nasty, and humiliating, as having someone spit in your face. Let's say you react just as many people would, and you give this guy a richly deserved punch in his face. Can you see any problems here? Well, two problems would quickly be apparent right after your brief retaliatory satisfaction. One, he's handcuffed and in custody. Two, you're a police officer. Oh, don't forget that there's going to be witnesses. With your luck, there'll be at least one camcorder in the crowd catching all the action. The problem with home video is that it's going to record your punch with much more clarity than the suspect's flying lugy. Think about the notoriety you'll achieve on the news at 11. Remember the suspect's swollen face? You know, the injury you inflicted on him during the initial battle. You'll see him display that injury during his televised interview claiming the injury was sustained from your unprovoked assault on him. For that matter, you'll be the subject of numerous television and print stories; until, something else knocks you off the front page.

...sympathize with you

The reason I chose this example is simple. Many people would sympathize with you for reacting as you did. Your fellow officers would not be critical of you or at least most wouldn't. Even people from the community who'd had a good view of the provocation would be silently, and I mean silently, in agreement with your response. What's the saying? Sympathy and $1.25 will get you a cup of coffee. In your case, that's true. In the suspect's case, sympathy is going to get him a lot more.

…send you to jail

Your pitifully small sympathy base will be dwarfed by his which will include the media, politicians, police executives, civil rights organizations, and an infinite number of attorneys standing in line to represent him in his civil case. There won't be any criminal case against your suspect, because the State will never prosecute him for his assaults on you. It gets worse. What you did was an assault, so you'll have the local prosecutor to deal with. The best you could hope for would be a plea bargain; unless, the State's Attorney wants to send you to jail to enhance his or her career and reelection. Even if you get some mercy from the local prosecutor, the Federal government might want to try you for civil rights' violations.

…doesn't want to be controlled

There's one very simple way to ensure you'll never exercise excessive force in any way, shape or manner. Never allow your emotions to control your physical response to anything. That's the simple part. The hard part is using any amount of force that is not going to be viewed by others as excessive. Most people have no idea how difficult it is to control any person, of any size, when that person doesn't want to be controlled. Even a person in handcuffs can be extremely dangerous and require two or more officers to maintain control of that person.

…completely overpowered

You've probably seen video of three, four, or even five officers piling on top of a combative suspect. Most people can't comprehend why a person would resist when so completely overpowered which is why most people see such piling on as excessive. There will be times when you'll be forced to strike a suspect; however, this should not be one of those times.

…won't let go

Some people will resist so violently that even five officers will have a difficult time bringing a person under control. Imagine being in a similar situation, and the suspect bites you on your wrist and won't let go. Your first instinct would be to beat the fool on the head; until, he lets go of your wrist. In reality, that's probably what you'd do The problem with striking the suspect on the head is the possibility of inflicting serious injury. As serious as a human bite can be, if the suspect suffers a serious head injury, your nasty and painful wrist injury will not justify your response.

…only on the limbs

Police officers have always been issued sticks as part of their basic equipment. Today, the nightstick, or baton, comes in a variety of lengths, shapes, and weights. Polymers have replaced the traditional wooden stick in most departments. Some departments may issue a light weight metal collapsible baton. Whatever kind of stick your department authorizes, you'll be trained to strike a combative suspect only on the limbs to prevent inflicting life threatening injuries. If you're issued a long stick, you'll probably be trained to hold the stick as you would a baseball bat to take a suspect's legs out from under him. If you ever hit anyone with a batter's swing, just pray that nobody is videotaping you.

…it won't do

Remember escalation of force? It's a fine theory, but it's still a theory. Whenever you resort to the use of your stick as your first force option, the first question thrown at you will be why you didn't respond first with pepper spray? The simple response is, "You had to be there." As logical as this response may be, it won't do. Your department may have very stringent reporting requirements for any use of force. You must be able to articulate, in writing, logical and convincing reasons why you chose and used the force in question.

…less than lethal force

The big thing these days is the less than lethal force weapons. The two most popular methods are the Taser Gun, and bean bags fired from a 12 gauge shotgun. The Taser Gun has pulled way out in front since the bean bags have proven deadly in a few instances. The Taser shoots two small probes attached by wires to the gun. Once the probes attach to the suspect, the officer can control bursts of high voltage electricity; until, the suspect is incapacitated. I can tell you from experience that the Taser works well on police officers who volunteer to be tased, but, then, so does pepper spray.

…know next to nothing

The Taser Gun is a good less than lethal force weapon which is going to perform as advertised. The problem with any less than lethal weapon is that many activists, politicians, and others, who know next to nothing about incapacitating dangerous people, think the Taser Gun is "the" alternative to deadly force in every conceivable situation. Put simply, there will be times when a Taser Gun will be the perfect tool under the right circumstances. Until you're issued your Star Trek Faser weapon, which will instantaneously stun your suspect into unconsciousness, you'll have to rely on your service pistol as your weapon of last resort.

...critics are proliferating

Just like any other force used by police officers, the use of the Taser Gun is increasingly coming under criticism. As safe as the weapon has proven to be, the critics are proliferating in pace with the increased use of the weapon. The more video images shown of unresisting suspects tased for simple non-compliance will only increase the criticism. It will be up to your department to establish and maintain guidelines for the use of any less than lethal force weapon, and it will be your responsibility to follow those guidelines. Remember, no use of force by you will ever be immune from the excessive label.

...may not be immediately appreciated

Even experienced officers can over react in stressful situations. As a new officer, you should be loath to interfere with the conduct of a more experienced officer. Your interference, in most cases, would be wrong; however, if you see another officer exerting excessive force, it is your duty to terminate such use of force. Your action may not be immediately appreciated, but it's the right and necessary thing to do.

20

Deadly Force

…to defend your life or the life of another

There are many people who could not, under any circumstances, take the life of another person. If you're one of those people, you definitely do not want to become a police officer. Conversely, no police department needs a person who just can't wait for the opportunity to shoot someone. Outside the firing range, the vast majority of police officers will never have to discharge their firearms. However, nearly every police officer will, on occasion, have to make the decision not to use deadly force.

Every police department has guidelines describing circumstances where an officer may discharge his or her firearm. Over the years, these guidelines have undergone changes. Today, aside from the range, your department may limit your use of firearms only to defend your life or the life of another.

…points a handgun at you

Defending your life or the life of another. Sounds pretty simple, doesn't it? Let's look at a scenario. You're chasing a shoplifting suspect through a crowded shopping mall. The suspect is about twenty feet in front of you when he suddenly turns and points a handgun at you. You're in a mall, so there are people all around you and others at greater distances, behind you and the suspect, who are going about their shopping oblivious to what's happening.

What do you do? Before you answer this question, let's look at some of the things you have to consider in the time it takes for the suspect to point and fire his weapon at you:

• Your weapon is still holstered. How many shots might the suspect be able to fire, before you're able to draw and fire your weapon?

• You're twenty feet from the suspect. Twenty feet is not a great distance, but it's not so close that you couldn't miss the suspect if you fire your weapon.

• A bullet travels in a straight line. If you fire and miss, what are the chances your bullet will strike an innocent person. For that matter, if the suspect shoots at you, his bullet will either hit you or possibly strike an innocent person.

• Is there cover available? Sorry, in this scenario, nothing is close enough to be of use to you.

• Can you retreat? If you retreat to either side of the mall, you could put bystanders in those areas into the suspect's line of fire.

…life is in imminent danger

Let's answer this question first. In this scenario, would you be justified in using deadly force against this suspect? The answer is a qualified yes. The suspect is pointing a gun at you, and your life is in imminent danger. If you were within three to seven feet of the suspect, the answer would be a definite yes since this is a kill distance in which you'd have little chance of survival; unless, you use deadly force.

Okay. You draw and fire your weapon. Your bullet strikes the suspect in the chest, and he goes down like a bag of rocks. The suspect never fires his weapon; your bullet doesn't pass through the suspect and endanger anyone else, and the whole thing is over in an instant. Congratulations! You're a modern day Wyatt Earp, and there are plenty of witnesses to affirm your heroic performance.

But, what if? What if…you miss the suspect, and your bullet strikes a child standing next to her mother two hundred feet down the mall? What if…it turns into a blazing gun battle, and multiple bullets from you and the suspect fly throughout the mall? What if…during the gun battle, the suspect takes a hostage? What if…the whole thing turns into a horrible, bloody nightmare? What if…you lose the gunfight?

…no room for error

The problem with using deadly force is that there is no room for error. The only right outcome is for your bullets to hit the suspect, and any stray bullets must not strike anyone else.

...another option

Let's look at another option in this scenario. It's unlikely that you'll be able to draw and fire your weapon, before the suspect fires his weapon. At twenty feet, you're not within the critical kill distance. You have no immediate available cover, but you can retreat. Yes, you could be placing others in the suspect's line of fire; however, in this scenario there will be people in any line of fire. Remember, the suspect was initially fleeing from you, and seeing you retreat could cause the suspect to continue his flight. If the suspect does fire at you, you'll be a moving target widening the distance between yourself and the suspect rather than being in a stationary position exchanging bullets at a shorter distance.

Unless the suspect is a total whack job, in all probability he will continue to flee. Question? Do you continue to pursue the suspect? Problem. If you continue the pursuit, and the suspect turns and fires at you, even from a significant distance, innocent bystanders will again be put in jeopardy. In the initial pursuit, you had no reason to believe the suspect was armed, and you were not knowingly placing others in danger. You now know the suspect is armed and dangerous by his displayed willingness to shoot it out with you.

...experience to believe

I think you get the idea. Scenarios, like this one, are helpful to get your mind working in the right direction, but no scenario will ever fully prepare you for confronting the real thing. You're probably thinking how in the world would you have time to consider all the things described in this scenario while a man is pointing a gun at you? You'll have to experience an imminent life threatening situation to believe, and understand, how fast your mind will work. In such circumstances, your mind is capable of processing information at speeds that would make the fastest computer on the planet slow by comparison.

...ridiculous questions

It's pretty amazing how many intelligent, well educated people are willing to ask some of the most ignorant, uninformed, and ridiculous questions when a police officer uses deadly force. I know you've heard some of them. "Why didn't he [officer] just shoot the gun out of the guy's hand?" "Why didn't he just shoot him in the leg?" When the weapon involved is a knife, the questions get even better. "Why did he have to shoot the guy...all he had was a knife? Aren't cops trained in hand to hand? He could have just taken the knife away from him."

...center mass

When you receive your firearm's training, you're going to be trained to always aim for center mass. Center mass simply means the torso of the suspect's body, because the torso is the largest target. You'll be trained to "double tap." Double tap means that you'll fire two rounds in quick succession in order to apply maximum stopping power. Can such use of force kill a person? It certainly can kill; however, killing the suspect is not the purpose of shooting for center mass. The purpose is to incapacitate the suspect, so he can no longer be a threat to you or others.

...fatal wound

Bullets are funny things. They do pretty much what they want to do once they hit something. You could fire your two bullets at center mass, and one bullet completely misses the suspect. The other bullet strikes the suspect in his shoulder, and the wound is fatal. Fatal? How could the wound be fatal? Modern firearms' ammunition travels at very high velocities. When a bullet hits bone, it's not uncommon for the bullet to change direction and travel along the bone. Therefore, a bullet shot into a person's arm can end up in the chest cavity piercing vital organs. Small caliber bullets are especially lethal in this regard. During your career, you may see a victim with an entry wound in the lower left back, and the exit wound at the top of the right shoulder. The victim may even be sitting up and talking to you, but you'll realize that, even with today's medical marvels, the odds are against that victim's survival.

...fantasy of the uninformed

Here's the point. If you're using deadly force, you're in the process of protecting your life or the life of another. You have to incapacitate the suspect as quickly as possible. Once you train with firearms, you'll understand that the idea of just shooting here or there to wound, or accomplish some other incredible feat, is just a fantasy of the uninformed. You'll also learn that the "double tap" is not always sufficient. Today, most departments issue officers high capacity handguns. A high capacity handgun is a semi-automatic pistol holding fifteen to seventeen rounds of ammunition versus the six round revolver of the past. In the past, officers have died at the hands of their suspects after the officers fired their guns empty.

…conduct an experiment

For some reason, a lot people, including police officers, don't view a suspect armed with a knife as threatening as one armed with a gun. I would suggest that you conduct an experiment with a friend. Since toy pistols are harder to find these days than real guns, locate an item that will approximate the size and weight of a handgun. Put the item in your belt, waistband, or pocket to resemble a holstered handgun. Instruct your friend to stand fifteen feet from you with his or her hand raised as though holding a knife. At a point of your friend's choosing, he or she will run toward you as fast as possible and plunge the imaginary knife into your chest.

As soon as you observe your friend's forward movement, you draw your fake gun; point it at your friend and say, "Bang." Now, you can't cheat on this. The fake gun must be pointing at your friend when you say, "Bang." Unless your friend is on crutches at the time of this experiment, you're going to be very surprised at the outcome. Once you conduct the knife experiment, go back to the original scenario and replace the suspect's gun with a knife. In the altered scenario, the suspect rushes you as your friend did. What would you do?

…under a microscope

If, as a police officer, you have to use deadly force, your decision and your implementation of that decision will be placed under a microscope. Others, in and out of your department, will examine every minute detail of the incident. If death results from your decision to use deadly force, that examination will only intensify. There will be nothing you can do after the fact to change what happened, so your basic rule must always be not to use deadly force unless to protect life.

…very dangerous world

Contrary to the belief of a whole lot of so called enlightened people, we all live in a very dangerous world. There are a lot of dangerous jobs where men and women risk accidental death or serious injury everyday, but they are rarely at risk of intentional injury or death at the hands of another human being. As a police officer, you'll always be the first one called to protect life, and you'll always be the first one criticized when life is lost. If you're the one who takes that life, you'd better make sure you're right about everything.

...the life of another

Protecting your life or the life of another sounds pretty straight forward. Actually, making a decision to protect your life is a lot less complicated than deciding to use deadly force to save the life of another person.

...not always as they appear to be

You'll soon learn that many situations involving life threatening actions by one person toward another can be problematic. Aside from the tactical decisions associated with deadly force, you'll have to make judgements based solely on your observations. Realizing that things are not always as they appear to be, your interpretations of your observations will literally determine life and death.

...you hear a woman screaming

Let's try another scenario. You're on patrol when you hear a woman screaming. You see a man and woman standing together in front of a chain link fence. The man has the woman pressed against the fence with one hand while he holds a knife in his other hand. The man is pressing the knife against the woman's very pregnant mid section.

The suspect sees you approaching in your marked police vehicle, yet he makes no attempt to flee. What does this tell you? It tells you that the suspect and victim are not strangers to one another, and the assault your witnessing is not a random act of violence. You position your vehicle to afford yourself protection as you exit and point your pistol at the suspect.

Needless to say, you are in a deadly force situation. Tactically, you're in pretty good shape. You have the protection of your vehicle to slow the suspect should he attack you. You're close enough to minimize the possibility of hitting the victim should you have to shoot. You order the suspect to drop the knife.

Well, you really didn't expect him to drop the knife, did you? You're going to find out just how many people are totally unimpressed by a police officer pointing a gun at them. This is where your judgement and interpretation of an event is so critical. Back to the scenario. The suspect is looking at you as he continues to point the knife at the woman's stomach. The suspect ignores a second order from you to drop his knife. To add to the flavor of this standoff, the woman is constantly screaming, "He's going to kill me! Do something...do something!"

What would you do? Would you shoot this suspect? In this real life scenario, I decided not to use deadly force. Throughout our confrontation, the suspect never took his eyes off me, and he never said a word. As I looked over the sights of my gun into the man's face, I mustered the calmest and most deliberate tone I could and said to him, "If you cut that woman, I'm going to kill you." It worked. After analyzing me for a few more seconds, he dropped the knife and surrendered.

…unsympathetic toward the victim

You might think my last command to the suspect was unsympathetic toward the victim, but you had to be there. Every deadly force situation is unique. In this actual incident, if I had said, "Drop the knife, or I'm going to kill you," what course of action would have been left to me if the man ignored a third demand from me to drop his knife? Being there means everything, and your perspective of the situation is the only thing that counts. Of course, your perspective has to be right. In this incident, I was relatively certain that the suspect would not harm the woman. He had ample opportunity to stab the woman and flee, or he could have stabbed the woman and then committed suicide by attacking me. When he first observed me, he could have simply fled, but fleeing from me would have exhibited cowardly behavior in what was a fairly obvious domestic assault. He chose to engage me in a standoff; until, I ended the standoff by forcing him to make the next move.

…"he didn't have no knife"

You might think the woman, whose life I had arguably saved, would have been somewhat appreciative…wrong. Moments earlier she was screaming to me, "Do something!" As I put handcuffs on the suspect, who was her boyfriend…big surprise, she began admonishing me for arresting her boyfriend, "He didn't do nothing…he didn't have no knife, and I'll testify to that!" Think what would have happened had I used deadly force against this suspect. I would have prevailed in the end, because, like all liars, this woman would have embellished her account of the events to the point where even the most zealous investigator or prosecutor would have had to throw in the towel.

…inability to have any individual control

Finding yourself in a deadly force situation by yourself can be a scary thing, and you might think being one of two or more officers present would be an advantage for you. From a psychological perspective that could be true, but the down side is your inability to have any individual control over unfolding events.

As a new officer, having other officers present could be an advantageous position for you or a disastrous one.

…criminal and civil jeopardy

If you're present where another officer employs deadly force unlawfully, or simply as a result of poor judgement, you're going to be in a terrible mess. Even if you're a brand new officer, you could find yourself in criminal and civil jeopardy for not acting to prevent the misuse of deadly force. It can get worse. If you blindly follow others and employ deadly force just because another, or others, are shooting, you're a fool, and you're going to pay the price. The decision for you to use deadly force is your choice and your choice alone.

…bad people driving automobiles

It's impossible to know what kind of deadly force situations you'll face during your career. Each one will be unique, but some will have similarities. During your conduct of business, you'll have countless encounters with bad people driving automobiles. If you stop a car, and the driver jumps out with a gun in his hand and starts shooting, your decision to respond with the same level of force would be a pretty easy decision to make. But, what if the driver simply puts the car in reverse and tries to strike you with the automobile as you're walking toward him or her?

…formidable and deadly weapon

If you're old enough to be a police officer, you're old enough to know that automobiles can make normal people abnormal. Perhaps it's the power of the internal combustion engine, combined with the armor like protection of the car's metal body, that sometimes takes a person's confidence level to extremes. A car can be a very formidable and deadly weapon in the hands of a person who has taken leave from his or her senses or in the hands of a person who is just desperate to get away from you.

…most difficult use of deadly force justification

The question is, when would a person's use of an automobile justify your use of deadly force to stop that person? The word *never* comes to mind; even though, one can never say never to the use of deadly force when a dangerous person is in possession of, and utilizing, any instrument of deadly force. If you're sufficiently confused, you should be, for shooting at a person utilizing no other weapon than the automobile he or she is operating is the most difficult use of deadly force justification you could ever attempt to make.

…feeling of indestructibility

At first glance, the most obvious and seemingly legitimate justification for shooting at a moving vehicle would be when the operator of that vehicle is trying to run you down. If you're a new officer, you're probably young, and youth does produce the feeling of indestructibility in all of us. However, taking a shooting stance and dueling with a ton or more of rolling metal really isn't a sensible or sane thing to do. Legs are made for walking…and running. The critical seconds you consume in discharging your firearm will only bring you seconds closer to serious injury or death. The only good way such a confrontation could end would be for you to miss the vehicle entirely, but the gunfire would frighten the driver so badly that he or she would stop the vehicle, before striking you, and surrender. Good luck.

…finality of your act cannot be overstated

The only way you can prepare yourself for deadly force situations is to think about the certainty that you will encounter them. When you find yourself in one, you might not have the greatest tactical advantage, but, at least, your mind won't be unprepared for the ordeal. You'll make many mistakes during your career, and as long as those mistakes are made in good faith, most will not impact negatively upon you. The one mistake which will never be forgiven is your misuse of deadly force. If you're unfortunate enough to have to take the life of another human being, the finality of your act cannot be overstated. Your training and good sense must be the only influences bearing on your decision to use deadly force.

21

The Mental Case

...mountain of muscles

You'll be on patrol, and your dispatcher will direct you to a location for the "Mental Case." The longer you're on the job the more you're going to hate hearing..."mental case." A mental case can range from a little, frail lady to a six foot four mountain of muscles with voices telling him to destroy everything in sight.

...protect life and property

Mental case is merely a generic term to warn you that you're responding to a potentially dangerous situation with a person who could be mentally unstable. Since you're not a mental health professional, you're not expected to medically diagnose a person's mental state. Your job is to protect life and property; however, unless you're really dense, you'll be able to determine whether or not the person's behavior is unusual. Depending on the your state's laws applicable to emergency commitments, you'll probably have some kind of procedure for taking a person into custody for a psychiatric evaluation when you observe that person display certain behaviors such as his or her intention to commit suicide.

...the fuse is still burning

The violent mental case should be self explanatory. You could arrive to find the violent mental case already on his or her rampage, or you could arrive while the fuse is still burning. You should never respond to any mental case call alone, and you should never attempt to subdue a violent mental case my yourself. This is easy to say. You could find yourself in a position where you won't have a choice other than to confront a violent mental case, but you want to do everything in your power to avoid that choice.

Most often, a really violent mental case is in his or her own world. Your first concern should be removing any people from the path, or immediate vicinity, of the mental case. For example, your mental case could be in a room destroying everything in sight and threatening to kill imaginary aggressors. This is one instance where it's not usually that difficult to get people to move. Even family members will normally follow your directions without question.

...overwhelming physical force

When the time comes to confront a violent mental case, that confrontation should only be executed with overwhelming physical force. Ideally, your mental case will stay confined to one area while preparations are made to safely subdue the mental case. Most departments will have shields and less than lethal weapons available for these types of situations. Some departments will have an emergency response unit, specifically trained and equipped for similar situations, available to assist you.

...seemingly passive mental case

There are a few things you should always keep in mind when you confront a seemingly passive mental case. First, get as much information as possible about the mental case from family members, or others, and then get them out of the way. When you confront the passive mental case, familiarize yourself with the immediate surroundings and identify objects that could be used as weapons. Never position yourself where the mental case can trap you denying you a route of escape. Hopefully, you'll have a back up officer with you who can keep his or her mouth shut and let you talk to the person. Never...ever...ever yell at these people. The surest way to make your mental case explode is to make him or her perceive you as threatening.

...never delude yourself

When you're talking with a passive mental case, never delude yourself into thinking you're in control. If your mental case is a foot taller than you and out-weighs you by fifty pounds, this assumption won't be a problem. However, when you're the physically larger presence, you could make this mistake. You're in control only as long as you can communicate with the mental case, and you can bring the incident to a conclusion without violence.

...would you really like to find out

You never want to fight a mental case one on one or even two on one. The mental case can exert physical strength far beyond anything you can imagine. The mental and physical state of a real mental case can be so extreme that even if you would shoot the person through the heart, that person could still kill you in the minute or two it would take for the person to bleed to death. Even if you shoot the person in the head, there is no guarantee the bullet would destroy the portion of the brain controlling the body's motor responses. Thankfully, a mental case this indestructible is rare, but would you really like to find out?

22

For Women Only

...enormous transformation

A little more than three decades ago, police departments underwent an enormous transformation. Never before had women been in uniform performing the same police duties as men. While departments employed women with the designation of "police woman," the duties of these women were limited to administrative functions and interaction with female prisoners. Obviously, positions for police women were severely limited, as compared to men, since their duties were restrictive, and the arrests of females were not in the abundance that they are today. A police woman's opportunity for promotion was bleak, because promotions were limited and rarely exceeded the first supervisory level.

...simply confused

When the transformation got underway, a lot of people were opposed to the idea of putting women on the street to catch bad guys. Many more people, women as well as men, were just simply confused. The vast majority of men, young as well as older, possessed a cultural mind set which wasn't all that compatible with the new reality. Many men, or perhaps even most, believed the transformation would be a short lived experiment.

...ill prepared

In the beginning, the flood gates remained in tact. Women were not exploiting the new career opportunity in vast numbers. It's a good thing, because police departments were ill prepared to handle the limited numbers of women who were seeking the new adventure.

…dainty little cap

Something as simple as the uniform was a problem. Utility demanded that the women be issued trousers, but many departments also issued skirts and a dainty little cap to maintain the woman's feminine identity. Well, needless to say, the skirts and caps didn't last that long. Today, you'll rarely, if ever, see a female officer attired differently from her male counterparts when in uniform.

…first thing to go

In the early 1970's, departments had minimum height and weight requirements for hiring new officers. Departments cited studies of the time showing that taller officers were assaulted less frequently than shorter officers. Departments required weight to be proportionate to height, and new applicants were required to pass minimum physical performance tests to measure strength and endurance. At the time, nearly all departments had a minimum height requirement of 5' 8". While the height requirement alone excluded many men, who otherwise were fully qualified to become police officers, it obviously excluded more female applicants when measured proportionately to men. Of course, the height requirement was the first thing to go. One only needs to now look at police officers, in most communities, to see that weight proportionate to height is also a thing of the past.

…assistance of men

The woman's safety was an early major concern. Female officers were spread around as much as possible. For example, if the district; precinct, etc. had only three women, each would be assigned to a different shift. If more than one woman were assigned to one shift, each would be assigned to a different squad. The thinking here was to afford the woman the assistance of men when she became involved in physically dangerous situations. Some views die hard. Even today, with the numbers of female officers sufficient to comprise the majority of a squad, they still remain as a significant minority in any tactically functioning unit.

…under pressure

Ask any police executive today, and he or she will tell you that a department's uniform patrol force is the "backbone" of the department. Sure. In actuality, it is the backbone, but patrol is rarely viewed or treated that way. A new officer's goal is to leave patrol as soon as possible and be assigned to a specialized unit. When women were first hired, police leadership was under political pressure to make this happen as soon as possible for at least some female officers.

…disgusting exhibition

In the beginning, a strange phenomenon occurred. Out of the limited number of females available for transfer to specialized assignments, only the most physically attractive women were considered to be the most qualified. What would you expect? Departments were totally male dominated. For many of us around at the time, it was a totally disgusting exhibition of men making fools of themselves. One cannot blame the women who benefitted from their good looks and mens' weakness for pretty women. It was just another circumstance added to a culture of favoritism which exists in any police organization.

…more baggage than benefit

In police departments today, men are still as weak as ever. The more attractive you are the more men there will be available to fall over themselves to make your job easier. However, if you let yourself succumb to this temptation, you'll end up with more baggage than benefit. If you're serious about a career as a police officer, you won't let yourself become dependent on male officers. Even the appearance of dependence will damage your career at some point. You should do as any man should. Make yourself knowledgeable and self sufficient.

While you shouldn't exploit men, even if they want to be exploited, don't go the other way either. The longer you work with male officers, the more you'll be treated like one of the boys. That treatment can be critical at times. Criticism of one another is the life blood of police officers. When your turn in the box comes, and it will, don't take it personally. Never let men you work with hear you say, "A woman has to do everything twice as good as a man." To men, this is probably the most offensive statement in the feminists' arsenal of hyperbole.

…can cause a lot of problems

Everybody knows that workplace romances exist, and many people meet their future spouses in the workplace. If this is the sole reason you're considering joining a police department, good luck. If you're serious about the job, be very careful about forming a personal relationship with another officer. A good relationship can be a wonderful thing, but, when a relationship goes bad, it can cause a lot of problems. Unlike other lines of work, your personal relationship(s) is under more scrutiny when you're a police officer.

…only so far

Thirty years ago, women had an edge purely because they were women. Thirty years is a long time, and women have already completed entire careers leaving many more behind at all levels of a department. In other words, the good looks will get a woman only so far. Women can now afford themselves the benefits of the same institutional networks that men utilize…friendships and political connections. Welcome to the real world, you'll find that equality isn't all it's cracked up to be.

23

Modern Community Policing

...community politics

I'm sorry. If you're expecting the normal cheerleading phrases for community policing, you're not going to see them here. The modern definition of community policing has more to do with community politics than policing. It's true that hundreds of millions of federal tax dollars have been pumped into police departments across the nation to further the cause of community policing. The problem with supposedly free money is the strings attached to that money.

...most important resource

Many police departments will maintain their own grant writing units to take advantage of any monies available. The more grants a department receives for community policing, the more politicians, and top police brass, can take credit for doing who knows what. This wouldn't necessarily be a bad thing if the prolific nature of community policing activities didn't strain a department's most important resource...people. When a department takes money for a particular program, it must adhere to certain requirements of that program. For instance, a group of officers assigned to a program may not be available to their own commander for other, more pressing, needs. The more a department embraces the vast expanse of community policing theories, fewer officers will be available for traditional police deployment.

...small vocal segments

When you become a police officer, you might be surprised to learn that the vast majority of the community really doesn't think that much about what you do. When people do interact with the police, individual police officers will form, or affect, their opinions of police more than any million dollar community policing program. Community policing is popular with small, vocal segments of any

96

community. These people are usually very critical of police while believing the police department is the only agency of government. They will expect the police to address every single circumstance affecting the community's quality of life. "Quality of life" is the single most important phrase associated with community policing, and it's the phrase most often cited when justifying the use of police officers outside of the traditional police deployment.

…new…new…new ideas

I've used the word traditional which is usually synonymous with a four letter word to enthusiastic proponents of modern community policing. Think about this for a moment. What is community policing? Community policing was traditional policing, before it became modern policing. Modern community policing experts would have you believe that without their new…new…new ideas, you wouldn't be able to function. The truth is, aside from technology, there are no new ideas. With all the side trips associated with community policing, your most important function will always be catching the bad guys.

…more probable than you think

Speaking of new ideas. A very popular one these days is to encourage a police officer to reside in the same neighborhood where he or she patrols. Some programs exist to offer police officers financial incentives to purchase a home in the neighborhood. Community policing says this is the only way to make a police officer care about the community he or she serves. If you're ever tempted to take such an offer, don't do it.

Think about this. You're on patrol, and you're dispatched to a 911 hang up. Now, it's true, you really will care about this one, because it's coming from the house next door to your house. You're very concerned, because the couple who live there are good friends; his or her spouse is close to your spouse, and their children play with your children. You think, one of the kids could have dialed 911 and hung up, or, worse, one of the adults called 911, and he or she was then prevented from completing the call.

You arrive at the home, and you immediately recognize the worst. You hear screaming and the unmistakable sounds of a struggle. The front door is locked, so you immediately kick in the door. You rush in only to find one of your good friends beating the hell out of your other good friend. Your orders, or pleas, for the them to stop are ignored. You step into the fray where the aggressor spouse promptly assaults you. While you attempt to subdue the aggressor spouse, the victim spouse, seeing you using force to subdue the aggressor, attacks you.

Don't laugh. It's more probable than you think. How do you think such a situation would affect your "quality of life," and that of your family, for the foreseeable future. Of course, when your friends get out of jail and retrieve their children from social services, they might stop by to thank you, but don't count on it.

…only true refuge

In the past, your department would not assign you to patrol the neighborhood in which you reside. Experienced police leadership recognized that your job was hard enough without increasing your exposure to needless compromising situations. Today, politicians and police executives profess their concern for the well being of police officers, yet they would deny you the only true refuge from a stressful and demanding job…your home.

…created unique refuges

Community policing has created unique refuges for police officers who quickly tire of police work. You'll see no shortage of young officers volunteering for community policing programs that can remove them from the more hazardous and stressful day to day aspects of the job. In years past, when a young officer realized he or she was not suited to be a police officer, resignation was the most logical and honorable course. Today, community policing programs provide like officers with an attractive alternative. While their value to the community as police officers may be questionable, their unavailability to their fellow officers is not in question.

…better served

If you're serious about being a police officer, you'll be better served by staying in the traditional patrol function where you'll actually learn police work. If you feel you're burned out after two years, do everyone a favor and resign.

24

The Media

...never trust anybody

There are some very nice people in the news business. Some of them even like police, and those who like police generally have a better understanding of your job than many of their counterparts. Others will be openly hostile toward you; their hostility will be a result of their general dislike of police and your authority, or their implied hostility will simply be rude and pushy behavior they exert toward just about everybody. Nice or nasty, you should never trust anybody from the media.

...army of citizen reporters

There are a lot of reasons why being a police officer in the 21st Century is much more difficult than it was thirty years ago. Chief among those reasons is the proliferation of media, and the technical advances which can give you fifteen minutes of fame or fifteen months of torment. While the internet has had enormous influence on print media, the internet is only one of many things advancing the coverage of television news. Specifically, the camcorder and cell phone camera has given television news an army of citizen reporters...or should I say recorders?

...always watching you

Your worst nightmare should be appearing on television doing something stupid, or worse, unlawful. There's one thing of which you can be certain; someone is always watching you. You'll never know how many times you're videotaped by someone as you go about your duties, or how many times someone has rushed to the television station with a video of you doing something which that someone deems to be newsworthy.

...action and scandal

Television news loves police for two reasons...action and scandal. On a slow news day, every television assignment editor prays for a good police story. While some editors would prefer a story of extraordinary police action with a positive outcome, none will turn away from a story of police misconduct with an extraordinarily bad outcome.

...wonder what hit you

When the media, print and television, pursues a story that impacts negatively upon police, they do so with the information at hand. If you ever become involved in one of these stories, you're going to wonder what hit you. Even when your actions are totally justified and reasonable, you're going to feel very lonely. Seldom will top police officials come to your defense and contradict information from biased sources. If, on the other hand, your actions are not justified, or simply questionable, those same top officials will be conducting the choir in the condemnation of your poor judgement.

...not perfect

The only way you can protect yourself from biased, or slanderous, news coverage is to first realize the existence of the danger. Secondly, always be right. Since you're obviously not perfect, you'll have to constantly strive to make fewer mistakes, for the fewer mistakes you make increases the odds immeasurably in your favor.

...will get in your way

There will be plenty of times when you'll have some level of contact with people from the media. Most of your contacts will result from the misfortunes of others. Crime scenes and accident scenes will be your most common contacts. Most reporters, and television news' crews, know the single most important rule of a crime scene...stay out. Accident scenes are different; media folks will get in your way just like everybody else. You'll see some officers go out of their way to unnecessarily obstruct the media's movement. If the media is not obstructing you, there is no reason for you to obstruct them.

…talking heads

Whenever any newsworthy event occurs, on scene police officers are the most logical people for reporters to approach. Nearly every department has a designated person, or unit, to dispense information to the media. You should always, politely, direct reporters to that person or unit. A good reporter rarely lets it go at that, and he or she may continue to engage you in conversation to gain as much information from you as possible. Never lose your temper with reporters who try to pump you for information; they're just doing their job. Besides, if you're at a really newsworthy scene, there will be enough high ranking police officers rushing to the scene to appear as talking heads.

…one slippery slope

Never talk to reporters "off the record." When a reporter asks you to speak off the record, he or she is telling you that whatever you say will be treated as confidential. That's all well and good, but a request for you to speak off the record should tell you that you might well be stepping onto one slippery slope. Sometimes a reporter will use this tactic while casting a wide net for anything interesting. Other times, the reporter will be working on a very specific item. In either circumstance, there is never any benefit to you in speaking off the record.

…ride with patrol officers

There may well come a time when your department will purposely put you in direct contact with a member(s) of the media. The "Ride-Along" program is permitted in many departments where interested citizens, or members of the media, can ride with patrol officers during their tours of duty. As a new officer, you shouldn't be subjected to this added burden, but stranger things will happen. If you are assigned a ride-along, you must realize that the person is not there to promote your best interests.

…too comfortable and complacent

If your ride-along is a reporter, you have to be particularly suspicious. When you're in close contact with a person for two to eight hours, there is the danger of becoming too comfortable and complacent. You should always view your ride-along as an interrogator and yourself as the one being interrogated. You have to be very careful not to give responses which could, in any way, be construed to contradict any of your department's policies or procedures.

…out of harm's way

While your ride-along will have signed a release of indemnity freeing the department of liability for his or her safety, that release is only good as long as you don't do something stupid. The safety of your ride-along, even a reporter, is ultimately your responsibility. If you find yourself in a dangerous, or potentially dangerous, situation, your first responsibility is to ensure that your ride-along is out of harm's way.

…fair and objective

Police and media have one very important thing in common; both are supposed to be fair and objective. Just as police officers aren't perfect, neither are members of the media. While one reporter will do his or her absolute best to fulfill the requirements of fairness and objectivity, another will go forward with an agenda and little regard for objectivity. The best way for you to avoid agendas, and other troublesome involvements, is to just keep your mouth shut.

978-0-595-38078-7
0-595-38078-6

Printed in the United States
68312LVS00008B/164